Developmental Exercises for
Rules for Writers

Seventh Edition

Wanda Van Goor

Prince George's Community College

Diana Hacker

Bedford/St. Martin's   Boston ◆ New York

Manufactured in the United States of America.

8   7   6   5

l   k   j   i

For information, write: Bedford/St. Martin's
75 Arlington Street, Boston, MA 02116
(617) 399-4000

ISBN-13: 978-0-312-67807-4

Preface for Instructors

The exercises in this book are specifically designed for developmental students. All have been classroom tested.

The exercises in each set are thematically linked, usually focusing on the achievements of a famous person or group—such as Harriet Beecher Stowe, Louis Braille, impressionist painters, Amelia Earhart, Jackie Robinson, or the Beatles—so that students are reading real prose on interesting topics rather than unrelated drill sentences.

Here are the principal features of *Developmental Exercises for Rules for Writers*, Seventh Edition.

Respectful of students' college status

Although the exercises vary in level of difficulty, all of them respect the age and experience of college students. Most exercises ask students to edit paragraphs and essays, not to fill in blanks or recopy whole sentences when only a word or two may need changing. Where possible, exercises encourage students to think about the impact of errors on readers and to choose revision strategies that produce effective, not just "correct," writing.

Written in connected discourse

Because nearly every exercise is a paragraph, an essay, or a set of numbered sentences that are connected in meaning, students learn to identify and revise problem sentences in realistic contexts. These connected discourse exercises mimic the process of revision as it occurs in real writing. In addition, they provide a rhetorical context to guide students as they select among revision strategies. When revising comma splices and fused sentences, for example, students will see that relying too heavily on the period and the semicolon results in dull, monotonous prose. They will begin to see the need for occasional subordination, and the rhetorical context will suggest just where subordination would be most effective.

"Guided practice" exercises

Most sections open with a guided practice exercise that gives students special help. Section codes (such as 21, 21c) in the margin identify problem sentences and tell students where in *Rules for Writers*, Seventh Edition, to look for explanations and revision strategies. Answers to these exercises appear in the back of the book.

Varied formats

Seldom will students be asked to do exactly the same thing in two consecutive exercises. Varied ways of working on a topic keep the task interesting. Sometimes students need only to circle the letter of the correct or clearer sentence in a pair of sentences; sometimes they choose between two words or phrases; frequently they edit, crossing out incorrect or confusing forms and adding handwritten revisions; occasionally they edit the same sentence in two different ways.

Many exercises provide hints for students, telling them, for example, that two of the ten sentences in a set are correct or that half of the sentences use a strategy, such as parallelism, correctly and the other half need revision.

Emphasis on reading

As they learn to edit the sentences and paragraphs in the exercises, students do a considerable amount of reading, and many exercises ask them to respond as readers. In an exercise on mixed constructions, for example, students are asked to discriminate between the easy-to-read and the hard-to-read sentences. Where possible, students are encouraged to think about meaning. "Which sentences are unclear?" an exercise on needed words asks. An exercise on adjectives and adverbs asks what the difference is between the sentences "Most slaves did not find their escape routes easy" and "Most slaves did not find their escape routes easily."

Cross-curricular content

Most exercises profile a person or group that students are likely to encounter in college courses across the curriculum: Mary Wollstonecraft, Albert Einstein, Martin Luther King Jr., Sacagawea, Mother Jones, and so on. Because many of these people overcame great obstacles to achieve their goals, their stories are often inspirational as well as informative.

Adaptable to a variety of teaching styles

You can use the exercises in a variety of ways. Instructors have used them successfully for homework or quizzes, for nongraded individual study, for class discussions, and for collaborative learning in small groups.

Acknowledgments

I am grateful to several people at Bedford/St. Martin's who were actively involved in the book's development and production. Bedford founder and former president Charles Christensen and current president Joan Feinberg helped plan the book. Executive editor Michelle Clark responded to the manuscript, offering intelligent suggestions and upbeat encouragement. Senior editor Barbara Flanagan has reworked the exercises through several editions, and editorial assistant Kylie Paul refined and updated many exercises for this edition. Production editor Kendra LeFleur guided our complex manuscript through production.

Thanks also go to Claire Seng-Niemoeller for designing the book's pages and to copyeditor Linda McLatchie for bringing consistency and clarity to the final manuscript.

Finally, since Diana Hacker will always be a part of my work on the exercises, I'd like to echo her words: "For their support and encouragement, we would like to thank our families, our colleagues at Prince George's Community College, and the many students over the years who have taught us that errors, a natural by-product of the writing process, are simply problems waiting to be solved."

Wanda Van Goor
Prince George's Community College

Introduction for Students

To learn any skill—whether snowboarding, tennis, CPR, Web design, or the electric guitar—takes practice. Writing well is no exception: In a college composition class, you will learn to write by writing, and you will learn to revise by revising.

Developmental Exercises for Rules for Writers, Seventh Edition, will sharpen your revision skills by giving you a great deal of controlled, yet realistic, practice. Let's say, for example, that you want to learn to identify and revise sentence fragments. Your first step is to read section 19 in *Rules for Writers*, Seventh Edition, and to study the flowchart on page 181. Then, keeping *Rules for Writers* open to section 19, work on Exercise 19-1 in *Developmental Exercises for Rules for Writers*. Exercise 19-1, a "guided practice," gives codes in the margin (such as 19a or 19c) next to any word group that is a fragment. In addition to alerting you where to look for fragments, the codes refer to specific rules in the text; if you have trouble identifying or fixing a particular fragment, you can consult *Rules for Writers* for help. When you have finished the exercise, you should check your answers. Answers to the guided practice exercises appear in the back of this book, beginning on page 181.

Once you have done the guided practice exercise, attempt the other exercises in the set; continue to refer to *Rules for Writers* when you run into trouble. You'll find that the rest of the exercises in a set vary in style and level of difficulty. In the set on fragments, for example, one exercise asks you to identify the complete sentence in a pair of word groups; another, presented in paragraph form, asks you to identify fragments and to think about possible revision strategies; and three other exercises give you practice in both identifying and revising fragments. Throughout the entire set of exercises, the subject you'll be reading about is the Beatles. Other exercise sets resemble the one on fragments. In those sets you will encounter a number of famous people you are likely to read about in other college classes: men and women such as Karl Marx, Harriet Beecher Stowe, Frederick Douglass, Albert Einstein, impressionist painters, and Amelia Earhart.

Wanda Van Goor
Prince George's Community College

Contents

Preface for Instructors   iii

Acknowledgments   v

Introduction for Students   vi

Clarity (effective sentences)

8-1	Active verbs: Guided practice	1
8-2	Active verbs	2
8-3	Active verbs	3
8-4	Active verbs: Guided review	4
9-1	Parallelism: Guided practice	5
9-2	Parallelism	6
9-3	Parallelism	7
9-4	Parallelism: Guided review	8
10-1	Needed words: Guided practice	9
10-2	Needed words	10
10-3	Needed words	11
10-4	Needed words: Guided review	12
11-1	Mixed constructions: Guided practice	13
11-2	Mixed constructions	14
11-3	Mixed constructions	15
11-4	Mixed constructions: Guided review	16
12-1	Misplaced and dangling modifiers: Guided practice	17
12-2	Misplaced modifiers	18
12-3	Misplaced and dangling modifiers	19
12-4	Misplaced and dangling modifiers: Guided review	20
13-1	Distracting shifts: Guided practice	21
13-2	Distracting shifts	22
13-3	Distracting shifts	23
13-4	Distracting shifts: Guided review	24
14-1	Emphasis: Guided practice	25
14-2	Emphasis	26
14-3	Emphasis	27
14-4	Emphasis: Guided review	28
15-1	Variety: Guided practice	29
15-2	Variety	30
15-3	Variety: Guided review	31

Review of 8–15: Clarity (effective sentences)   32

Clarity (word choice)

16-1	Wordy sentences: Guided practice	33
16-2	Wordy sentences	34
16-3	Wordy sentences	35
16-4	Wordy sentences: Guided review	36
17-1	Appropriate language: Guided practice	37
17-2	Appropriate language	38
17-3	Appropriate language	39
17-4	Appropriate language: Guided review	40
18-1	Exact words: Guided practice	41
18-2	Exact words	42
18-3	Exact words	43
18-4	Exact words	44
18-5	Exact words: Guided review	45
	Review of 16–18: Clarity (word choice)	46

Grammar

19-1	Fragments: Guided practice	47
19-2	Fragments	48
19-3	Fragments	49
19-4	Fragments	50
19-5	Fragments	51
19-6	Fragments: Guided review	52
20-1	Run-on sentences: Guided practice	53
20-2	Run-on sentences	55
20-3	Run-on sentences	57
20-4	Run-on sentences	58
20-5	Run-on sentences: Guided review	59
21-1	Subject-verb agreement: Guided practice	60
21-2	Subject-verb agreement	61
21-3	Subject-verb agreement	62
21-4	Subject-verb agreement: Guided review	63
22-1	Pronoun-antecedent agreement: Guided practice	64
22-2	Pronoun-antecedent agreement	65
22-3	Pronoun-antecedent agreement	66
22-4	Pronoun-antecedent agreement: Guided review	67
23-1	Pronoun reference: Guided practice	68
23-2	Pronoun reference	69
23-3	Pronoun reference	70
23-4	Pronoun reference: Guided review	71
24-1	Pronoun and noun case: Guided practice	72
24-2	Pronoun and noun case	73
24-3	Pronoun and noun case	74
24-4	Pronoun and noun case: Guided review	75
25-1	*Who* and *whom*: Guided practice	76
25-2	*Who* and *whom*	77
25-3	*Who* and *whom*	78

25-4	*Who* and *whom*: Guided review	79
26-1	Adjectives and adverbs: Guided practice	80
26-2	Adjectives and adverbs	81
26-3	Adjectives and adverbs	82
26-4	Adjectives and adverbs: Guided review	83
27-1	Verb forms: Guided practice	84
27-2	Verb forms	85
27-3	Verb forms	86
27-4	Verb forms: Guided review	87
27-5	Verb tense and mood: Guided practice	88
27-6	Verb tense and mood	89
27-7	Verb tense and mood	90
27-8	Verb tense and mood: Guided review	91
	Review of 19–27: Grammar	92

Multilingual Writers and ESL Challenges

28-1	ESL verb use: Guided practice	93
28-2	Verb forms	94
28-3	Helping verbs, main verbs, and omitted verbs	95
28-4	Verb forms	96
28-5	Passive verbs	97
28-6	Conditional verbs	98
28-7	Verbs followed by gerunds or infinitives	99
28-8	Verbs followed by gerunds or infinitives	100
28-9	ESL verb use: Guided review	101
29-1	Articles: Guided practice	102
29-2	Articles	103
29-3	Articles	104
29-4	Articles: Guided review	105
30/31-1	Sentence structure, prepositions, and idiomatic expressions: Guided practice	106
30/31-2	Omissions and needless repetitions	107
30/31-3	Present and past participles	108
30/31-4	Placement of adjectives	109
30/31-5	Sentence structure, prepositions, and idiomatic expressions: Guided review	110
	Review of 28–31: Multilingual Writers and ESL Challenges	112

Punctuation

32/33-1	The comma and unnecessary commas: Guided practice	113
32/33-2	The comma	115
32/33-3	The comma	116
32/33-4	The comma	117
32/33-5	Unnecessary commas	118

32/33-6	Unnecessary commas	119
32/33-7	The comma and unnecessary commas: Guided review	120
34-1	The semicolon: Guided practice	121
34-2	The semicolon	122
34-3	The semicolon	123
34-4	The semicolon: Guided review	124
35-1	The colon: Guided practice	125
35-2	The colon	126
35-3	The colon	127
35-4	The colon: Guided review	128
36-1	The apostrophe: Guided practice	129
36-2	The apostrophe	130
36-3	The apostrophe	131
36-4	The apostrophe: Guided review	132
37-1	Quotation marks: Guided practice	133
37-2	Quotation marks	134
37-3	Quotation marks	135
37-4	Quotation marks: Guided review	136
38-1	End punctuation: Guided practice	137
38-2	End punctuation	138
38-3	End punctuation: Guided review	139
39-1	Other punctuation marks: Guided practice	142
39-2	Other punctuation marks	143
39-3	Other punctuation marks	144
39-4	Other punctuation marks: Guided review	145
Review of 32–39: Punctuation		146

Mechanics

40/41/42-1	Abbreviations, numbers, and italics: Guided practice	147
40/41/42-2	Abbreviations and numbers	148
40/41/42-3	Italics (underlining)	149
40/41/42-4	Abbreviations, numbers, and italics: Guided review	150
43/44/45-1	Spelling, the hyphen, and capitalization: Guided practice	151
43/44/45-2	Spelling	152
43/44/45-3	The hyphen	153
43/44/45-4	Capitalization	154
43/44/45-5	Spelling, the hyphen, and capitalization: Guided review	155
Review of 40–45: Mechanics		156

Grammar Basics

46-1	Parts of speech: Preview	157
46-2	Nouns and noun/adjectives	158
46-3	Nouns and noun/adjectives	159
46-4	Pronouns and pronoun/adjectives	160

46-5	Verbs	161
46-6	Adjectives and adverbs	162
46-7	Prepositions	163
46-8	Prepositions and conjunctions	164
46-9	Parts of speech: Review	165
47-1	Sentence patterns: Preview	166
47-2	Subjects	167
47-3	Direct objects and subject complements	168
47-4	Indirect objects and object complements	169
47-5	Direct objects, indirect objects, and object complements	170
47-6	Sentence patterns: Review	171
48-1	Subordinate word groups: Preview	172
48-2	Prepositional phrases	173
48-3	Prepositional and verbal phrases	174
48-4	Verbal phrases	175
48-5	Subordinate clauses	176
48-6	Subordinate word groups: Review	177
49-1	Sentence types: Preview	178
49-2	Sentence types	179
49-3	Sentence types: Review	180

Answers to Guided Practice and Preview Exercises   181

EXERCISE 8-1 ◆ Active verbs: Guided practice

Revise any weak or unemphatic sentences by replacing passive verbs or *be* verbs with active alternatives. The numbers in the margin refer to relevant rules in section 8 of *Rules for Writers*, Seventh Edition. The first revision has been done for you; a suggested revision of this exercise appears in the back of this book.

Young slave Frederick Douglass enjoyed indulging

~~Indulging~~ in his favorite fantasy about slave owners. ~~was something that young~~   8b

~~slave Frederick Douglass enjoyed.~~ In his fantasy, everyone was in a conspiracy against   8b

the slave owners. No hint of a planned escape was given by slaves still in bondage.   8a

Members of the community never revealed the whereabouts of escaped slaves. Slaves

who escaped successfully never talked too much about how they got away. Owners

were told nothing at all by slaves they recaptured. Even some white southerners who   8a

sympathized with the slaves gave no information to their slave-owning friends. The

part of his fantasy that Douglass enjoyed most was the final part. In it, Douglass   8b

imagined slave owners as being too afraid to hunt escaping slaves. The owners were   8b

distrustful of their slaves, their enemies, and even their friends.

Van Goor and Hacker, *Developmental Exercises for Rules for Writers*, 7th ed. (Boston: Bedford, 2012)

8-1 | Active verbs: Guided practice   **1**

EXERCISE 8-2 ♦ Active verbs

To read about this topic, see section 8 in *Rules for Writers*, Seventh Edition.

In the following paired sentences, circle the letter of the sentence in which the verbs are active and emphatic. Be ready to explain your choice. Example:

a. On his second attempt, Frederick was able to escape by pretending to be a sailor.

(b.) On his second attempt, Frederick escaped slavery by pretending to be a sailor.

1. a. The use of another man's sailing papers was the way Frederick got to Philadelphia.
   b. Frederick used another man's sailing papers to get to Philadelphia.

2. a. He did not even consider the possibility of staying in Philadelphia.
   b. The possibility of staying in Philadelphia was not even considered by him.

3. a. In Philadelphia, he asked the first black man he saw how to get to New York.
   b. In Philadelphia, the first black man he saw was asked how to get to New York.

4. a. Arriving in New York was what made Frederick feel safe.
   b. Arriving in New York made Frederick feel safe.

5. a. Luckily, a sympathetic abolitionist found Frederick before a slave catcher could find him.
   b. Luckily, Frederick was found by a sympathetic abolitionist before a slave catcher could find him.

Van Goor and Hacker, *Developmental Exercises for Rules for Writers*, 7th ed. (Boston: Bedford, 2012)

EXERCISE 8-3 ◆ Active verbs

To read about this topic, see section 8 in *Rules for Writers*, Seventh Edition.

Half of the following sentences contain passive verbs or verbs that are a form of *be*. Find them and change them to active verbs. You may need to invent a subject for some verbs, and you may need to make major revisions in some sentences. If a sentence already contains only active verbs, mark it as "active." Example:

> *P*
> ~~Frederick Douglass was annoyed by~~ people who spoke openly of helping the underground
>   *annoyed Frederick Douglass.*
> **railroad/**
>   ^

1. Douglass said that by talking openly about it, these people had turned the "underground railroad" into an "upperground railroad."

2. Although these people were deserving of praise, their open talk endangered escaping slaves.

3. Such talk alerted slave owners to possible escape routes.

4. Escaping slaves would often be caught by professional slave hunters at the houses of those who talked openly.

5. All slaves were threatened by any information that increased slave owners' knowledge.

6. Whenever slave owners suspected some of the escape routes, the courage of the slaves was lost.

7. Frederick Douglass understood the slaves' fears very well: His first attempt to escape had failed.

8. Professional slave breakers beat and tortured captured slaves until the slaves submitted or died.

9. His own treatment at the hands of slave breakers left Douglass with severe, disfiguring scars all over his back.

10. Years later, northerners were convinced by those scars that Douglass spoke the truth about slavery.

Van Goor and Hacker, *Developmental Exercises for Rules for Writers*, 7th ed. (Boston: Bedford, 2012)

8-3 | Active verbs   3

EXERCISE 8-4 ◆ Active verbs: Guided review

Revise any weak or unemphatic sentences by replacing passive verbs or *be* verbs with active verbs. The numbers in the margin refer to relevant rules in section 8 of *Rules for Writers*, Seventh Edition. The first revision has been done for you.

                      changed some of his

~~Some of~~ Frederick Douglass's ideas about the North ~~were changed~~ after his   8a

successful escape from slavery. Before that time, Douglass's assumption was that   8b

northerners lacked both money and culture. In the South, only poor people owned

no slaves. Also, no lovely homes, no pianos, no art, and often no books were owned by   8a

poor people. When he first saw New Bedford, Massachusetts, Douglass was doubtful of   8b

his own eyesight. He saw no dilapidated houses or naked children or barefoot women

in New Bedford. Instead, the beautiful homes with equally beautiful furniture and

gardens were an indication of considerable wealth. Quality merchandise was handled   8b, 8a

by laborers on the wharves and purchased by them in the stores. When he saw all of

this, Douglass happily changed his ideas about the North.

Van Goor and Hacker, *Developmental Exercises for Rules for Writers*, 7th ed. (Boston: Bedford, 2012)

EXERCISE 9-1 ◆ Parallelism: Guided practice

Edit the following paragraphs to correct faulty parallelism. The numbers in the margin refer to relevant rules in section 9 of *Rules for Writers*, Seventh Edition. The first revision has been done for you; a suggested revision of this exercise appears in the back of this book.

In his own time, one famous sixteenth-century Italian was known only by his given name, Leonardo. Today he is still known by that single name. But then and now, his name suggests many different roles: biologist, botanist, inventor, engineer, strategist, researcher, and artist.

Sixteenth-century Venetian soldiers knew Leonardo as a military strategist. When the Turkish fleet was invading their country, Leonardo suggested conducting surface underwater attacks and ~~to flood~~ *flooding* the land that the Turkish army had to   9b
cross. Engineers knew him as the man who laid out new canals for the city of Milan. Scientists admired him for not only his precise anatomical drawings but also for his   9b
discovery that hardening of the arteries could cause death. To Milan's royal court, Leonardo was the artist who was painting impressive portraits, sculpting a bronze horse memorial to the house of Sforza, and at the same time worked on a mural of the   9a
Last Supper.

Leonardo saw a three-dimensional *s*-curve in all of nature—the flow of water, the movements of animals, and how birds flew. We recognize the same *s*-curve today   9a
in the spiraling form of DNA. Leonardo invented the wave theory: He saw that grain bending as the wind blew over it and water rippling from a stone dropped into it were the same scientific event. It was as easy for him to see this wave in sound and light as observing it in fields and streams. The math of his day could not explain all his   9b
theories, but twentieth-century scientists showed the world that Leonardo knew what he was talking about.

Leonardo saw very clearly that the powers of nature could be destructive and human beings could be savage. At the same time, he saw a unity holding all of life's   9c
varied parts together, a unity he could express in his art.

Leonardo—it's quite a name!

EXERCISE 9-2 ◆ Parallelism

To read about this topic, see section 9 in *Rules for Writers*, Seventh Edition.

All of the following sentences make an attempt to use parallel structure. Half of them succeed. The other five need revision. Put "OK" by the correct ones, and edit the other five to correct faulty parallelism. Example:

> **Leonardo spent the first years of his life playing in the fields, drawing animals and plants,**
>   *building*
> **and ~~he built~~ miniature bridges and towers along the river.**
>   ^

1. When Leonardo moved to Florence to live with his father, he exchanged a slow-moving rural life for a fast-paced urban one.

2. Because his birth parents had not been married, many job opportunities were not available to Leonardo. He could not become a merchant, a banker, or a skilled craftsman.

3. It was no easier for Leonardo to attend the local university than learning a craft.

4. The obvious choices were to become a soldier or he could join the priesthood.

5. Leonardo did not want his future to be in either the church or the army.

6. Deciding that Leonardo could draw better than he could march or pray, his father placed him with a major artist, Andrea del Verrocchio.

7. Verrocchio's shop worked for all kinds of customers, including trade unions, churches, and they would work for individuals also.

8. Living in Verrocchio's home and working in his shop, Leonardo heard talk of new theories about geography and science while he learned skills like modeling, painting, and sculpture.

9. Perhaps even more important was the variety of instruments Leonardo learned to make, among them musical, navigational, and ones for surgeons to use.

10. Working with Verrocchio was like going to three schools: an art school, a technology institute, and a liberal arts college.

Van Goor and Hacker, *Developmental Exercises for Rules for Writers*, 7th ed. (Boston: Bedford, 2012)

EXERCISE 9-3 ♦ Parallelism

To read about this topic, see section 9 in *Rules for Writers*, Seventh Edition.

Circle the letter of the word or word group that best completes the parallel structure in each sentence. Example:

> **Leonardo was handsome, generous, clever, and _____.**
> **a.) ambidextrous**
> **b. able to use either hand for most activities**
> **c. he could use either hand for most activities**

1. Leonardo's life had three distinct periods: his childhood in Vinci, his apprenticeship in

   Florence, and _____ .

   a. when he was an adult

   b. his being an adult and earning his own way

   c. his adulthood in various Italian cities

2. In childhood, Leonardo had not only a loving family and relatives but also _____ .

   a. safe and unspoiled acres to explore

   b. he had the whole gentle slope of a mountain to explore

   c. including fields and vineyards to explore

3. However, two natural events haunted his memory for years: A hurricane destroyed much of

   the valley below his village, and _____ .

   a. a flood washed away much of the city of Florence

   b. a flood that washed away much of the city of Florence

   c. the boiling, muddy, surging waters of a flood

4. Wind and water became major topics for Leonardo's study. He decided that wind and water

   were both useful and _____ .

   a. did harmful things

   b. they caused harm

   c. harmful

5. Viewers can find in many of Leonardo's works small round pebbles washed by a stream,

   riverbanks covered with moss and flowers, and _____ .

   a. little freshwater crabs partly hidden beneath rocks

   b. viewers can find small freshwater crabs under rocks

   c. little freshwater crabs sometimes hide beneath rocks

Van Goor and Hacker, *Developmental Exercises for*
Rules for Writers, 7th ed. (Boston: Bedford, 2012)

9-3 | Parallelism   **7**

EXERCISE 9-4 ◆ Parallelism: Guided review

Edit the following paragraphs to correct faulty parallelism. The numbers in the margin refer to relevant rules in section 9 of *Rules for Writers*, Seventh Edition. The first revision has been done for you.

Leonardo's vision of life as one borderless unity affected both his personal life and ~~it affected~~ his artistic work.   9b

Leonardo did not simply look at the world; he studied it carefully. Watching the wind ripple the water in a pond, he was observant, intent, and in a serious mood. Leonardo saw no boundaries in nature; to him, people and animals were parts of one creation. He ate no meat because he did not want to bring death to a fellow creature; he bought caged songbirds so that he could set them free. Having no family of his own, he adopted a boy from another family to be both his son and he would be his heir. Even right- and left-handedness were the same to him. He filled his notebooks with mirror writing, but he wrote letters, reports, and proposals in the usual way. When his right hand became crippled, he used his left.   9a

                                                                        9b

Leonardo's view of all of life as one creation led him to artistic innovations. Before Leonardo, artists had always used outlines to separate a painting's subject from its background. Because Leonardo saw everything in nature as interrelated, he decided that using shadow and gradation of light and color was better than to use an outline. He wanted one thing to flow into another the way smoke flows into air. Looking at Mona Lisa's hand, for instance, viewers can find no line where one finger ends and the next one begins; the separation is done totally with shadows. This unified vision of the world affected the content of his paintings as well as the technique. Background and subject often echo each other in a picture: The drapery and folds of the subject's clothing may reflect background scenes of curving vines or rocky hills or water that flows.   9b

                                                                        9a

Leonardo recognized the great diversity surrounding him, but he believed that an even greater unity supported the diversity and his own work was an expression of that unity.   9c

Van Goor and Hacker, *Developmental Exercises for Rules for Writers*, 7th ed. (Boston: Bedford, 2012)

EXERCISE 10-1 ◆ Needed words: Guided practice

Add any words needed for grammatical or logical completeness in the following paragraphs. The numbers in the margin refer to relevant rules in section 10 of *Rules for Writers*, Seventh Edition. The first revision has been done for you; a suggested revision of this exercise appears in the back of this book.

Mary Wollstonecraft, an eighteenth-century writer, may have been England's first feminist. Her entire life reflected her belief in equal rights for women in all areas of their lives: personal, intellectual, and professional.

From childhood, she never had and never would accept the idea that men were   10a
accepted
superior to women. As a young girl, she knew that her drinking and gambling father deserved less respect than her long-suffering mother did. As an adult, she demanded that society give her the same freedom it gave men.

Wollstonecraft also demanded men pay attention to her ideas. She did not argue   10b
about an idea. Instead, she gave an example of what she objected to and invited her readers to think about it from various points of view. Working this way, she made few enemies among intellectuals. Indeed, she was attracted and respected by some of the   10a
leading intellectuals of her day. Among them she was as well known on one side of the Atlantic as on the other. Thomas Paine, the American orator and writer, probably knew her better than Samuel Johnson, the English writer.   10c

Professionally, she was a governess, teacher, and author. When her father's   10d
drinking destroyed the family, she and her sisters started a girls' school. Eventually, financial problems forced the school to close, but not before Mary had acquired enough firsthand experience to write *Thoughts on the Education of Daughters* (1786). As competent or more competent than other writers of the day, she was a more persuasive   10c
advocate for women than most other writers were.

Modern feminists may find it ironic that current encyclopedia entries for "Wollstonecraft" refer researchers to "Godwin," her married name—where they will find her entry longer than the entry for her famous husband, William Godwin.

EXERCISE 10-2 ◆ Needed words

To read about this topic, see section 10 in *Rules for Writers*, Seventh Edition.

Circle the letter of the clearer sentence in each pair—the sentence that contains all words needed for logical or grammatical completeness. Example:

> **a.** **Mary Wollstonecraft felt a woman did not have to marry a man in order to live with him.**
>
> **(b.)** **Mary Wollstonecraft felt that a woman did not have to marry a man in order to live with him.**

1. a. She never married, or wanted to, her first suitor.

   b. She never married, or wanted to marry, her first suitor.

2. a. With Gilbert Imlay, she discovered that travel could teach her much about the business world.

   b. With Gilbert Imlay, she discovered travel could teach her much about the business world.

3. a. She had a more intellectual relationship with William Godwin than Gilbert Imlay.

   b. She had a more intellectual relationship with William Godwin than with Gilbert Imlay.

4. a. In one way, she may have been as conservative as, if not more conservative than, other women of her day.

   b. In one way, she may have been as conservative, if not more conservative, than other women of her day.

5. a. Marrying Godwin when she became pregnant may have shown that she believed in and acted by society's rules for pregnant women.

   b. Marrying Godwin when she became pregnant may have shown that she believed and acted by society's rules for pregnant women.

Van Goor and Hacker, *Developmental Exercises for Rules for Writers*, 7th ed. (Boston: Bedford, 2012)

EXERCISE 10-3 ◆ Needed words

To read about this topic, see section 10 in *Rules for Writers*, Seventh Edition.

Missing words make some of the following sentences unclear. Add the needed words so that only one meaning is possible. If a sentence is clear as written, mark it "OK." Example:

did.

Mary Wollstonecraft approved of the French Revolution more than Edmund Burke /
^

1. Wollstonecraft blamed women's problems on the structure of society more than the men of her time.

2. Her ideas about women frightened other people less than her husband.

3. One of her daughters, Mary Shelley, who wrote *Frankenstein*, became as famous as Wollstonecraft herself.

4. The readers Mary Shelley attracted were different from those who enjoyed her mother's work.

5. Modern readers know Mary Shelley better than Mary Wollstonecraft.

Van Goor and Hacker, *Developmental Exercises for Rules for Writers,* 7th ed. (Boston: Bedford, 2012)

10-3 | Needed words **11**

EXERCISE 10-4 ◆ Needed words: Guided review

Add any words needed for grammatical or logical completeness in the following paragraphs. The numbers in the margin refer to relevant rules in section 10 of *Rules for Writers*, Seventh Edition. The first revision has been done for you.

                            that

    Most people in her era found ⌃ Mary Wollstonecraft used very persuasive tech-   10b

niques. She did not argue and never had by directly attacking those who disagreed   10a

with her.

    More astute than other women of her day, she used anecdotal "observations."

She knew that a story or anecdote would make her point best. Since she did not argue,   10d

her listeners never felt they had to defend their own positions and were able to listen

to her stories with reasonably open minds. The stories, which often made clever use

of allegory and metaphor, came from her own experience and observation. Preferring

examples from dressmaking to other occupations, she chose stories that illustrated her   10c

points and let the anecdotes speak for themselves. Her technique was as convincing, or   10c

more convincing than, outright argument.

    Mary Wollstonecraft's sense of timing was also good. In 1790, she wrote a

pamphlet entitled *A Vindication of the Rights of Men*. Part of her reason for writing

it was to respond to the excitement caused by the French Revolution (1789–1799).

People liked her pamphlet very much. While enthusiasm was still high, she produced

A Vindication of the Rights of Women in 1792. It, too, was well received.

    No doubt part of Mary Wollstonecraft's unusually effective writing came from

the fact that she not only believed in but also lived the ideas she wrote about.   10a

Van Goor and Hacker, *Developmental Exercises for Rules for Writers*, 7th ed. (Boston: Bedford, 2012)

EXERCISE 11-1 ♦ Mixed constructions: Guided practice

Edit the following paragraphs to eliminate problems with mixed constructions. The numbers in the margin refer to relevant rules in section 11 of *Rules for Writers*, Seventh Edition. The first revision has been done for you; a suggested revision of this exercise appears in the back of this book.

Sometimes it's hard to separate history from folklore. Casey Jones, John Henry, Johnny Appleseed, Uncle Sam—which of these ~~names~~ were real men? Although we've heard their stories, but are those stories true?

11b

11a

There really was a railroad engineer called Casey Jones; the reason he got that nickname was because of Cayce, Kentucky, where he lived as a boy. There really was a Cannonball too; it was the Illinois Central's fast mail and passenger train. There really was a wreck of Engine No. 382, and Casey died while slowing the train to save his passengers. Legend has it that when workers found his body in the wreckage, his hand was still on the air-brake lever. (The use of air brakes had recently been installed on trains to increase their braking power.)

11c

11b

John Henry was an African American railroad worker of great strength. In legend and song, he died after a timed contest against a steam drill. By using a hammer in each hand made John Henry win the contest. He drilled two holes seven feet deep; the steam drill bored only one nine-foot hole. The real John Henry died on the job, crushed by rocks that fell from the ceiling of a railroad tunnel.

11a

John Chapman, better known as Johnny Appleseed, was a wealthy and well-liked nurseryman who kept moving his place of business west as the frontier moved west. His boyhood friend Sam Wilson supplied meat to the US troops during the War of 1812. A worker told a government inspector that the "US" stamped on the meat stood for "Uncle Sam." Although it was a joke, but it caught on, and Congress made the "Uncle Sam" identification official in the 1960s.

11a

Van Goor and Hacker, *Developmental Exercises for
Rules for Writers*, 7th ed. (Boston: Bedford, 2012)

11-1 | Mixed constructions: Guided practice **13**

EXERCISE 11-2 ◆ Mixed constructions

To read about this topic, see section 11 in *Rules for Writers*, Seventh Edition.

Correct the mixed constructions in the following sentences. Example:

> **What European first set eyes on America? If you say Amerigo Vespucci, from whom the name "America" is said to derive, so̶ you'll be only half right.**

1. Although Vespucci claimed to have found a new continent, but there is no evidence that he ever reached any land in the Western Hemisphere.

2. Columbus may have seen parts of the Americas first, but when a German mapmaker believed Vespucci's claim and put Vespucci's name on the map explains why the lands became known as America.

3. If Vespucci wasn't the first European to find land across the Atlantic, so who was?

4. For most British historians who have worked on the question say that John Cabot got there first.

5. Early mariners, a very dangerous occupation, often sailed under several names.

6. John Cabot was the name for Italian mariner Giovanni Caboto used when he worked for the English.

7. Some people say that Leif Eriksson saw the coast of North America first; their reason is because he established a small community on Newfoundland about AD 1000.

8. Even though Eriksson's community was established five hundred years before the time of Vespucci, Columbus, and Cabot, but the Norse sagas claim that Bjarni Herjulfsson sighted North America before Eriksson did.

9. The growth in the number of theories increases as new evidence is found.

10. So who was the first European on American shores? As these bits of history indicate that no one can really answer that question.

Van Goor and Hacker, *Developmental Exercises for Rules for Writers*, 7th ed. (Boston: Bedford, 2012)

EXERCISE 11-3 ◆ Mixed constructions

To read about this topic, see section 11 in *Rules for Writers*, Seventh Edition.

Read through each sentence just once. If it sounds correct to you, put "OK" after it. If it sounds like a mixed construction, put "MC" after it. Then go back and check; only four of the sentences should have "OK" after them. Fix the others. Example:

> **Do you believe that ~~because of~~ Paul Revere's late-night horseback ride alerted Minutemen from Boston to Lexington to Concord that the British were coming?** ___*MC*___

1. In college, most American students discover that their knowledge of history is a mixture of fact and fiction. _____

2. For example, most students believe that Paul Revere rode alone, alerting citizens from Boston to Concord that the British were coming. In fact, Revere did not ride alone, and he never made it to Concord. _____

3. Since he was able to borrow a horse permitted Revere to get as far as Lexington. _____

4. By adding two other riders, William Dawes and Samuel Prescott, made it possible to get the warning to Concord. _____

5. The vigilance of a group of British soldiers on patrol overtook all three men, captured Revere, and found out who he was. _____

6. The reason Minutemen reported promptly for duty was because they were warned by relays of riders who had been alerted by prearranged signals. _____

7. If Henry Wadsworth Longfellow had not written a poem about the ride forty-five years after Revere's death, so Revere might never have become famous. _____

8. Before that poem appeared, Paul Revere's name was not on any list of important people in America. _____

9. The increase in the number of times his name appeared on such lists after the poem was published was enough to make him famous. _____

10. Is fiction more powerful than fact? Is all our knowledge such a mixture of fact and fiction? _____

Van Goor and Hacker, *Developmental Exercises for Rules for Writers*, 7th ed. (Boston: Bedford, 2012)

11-3 | Mixed constructions   **15**

EXERCISE 11-4 ◆ Mixed constructions: Guided review

Edit the following paragraphs to eliminate problems with mixed constructions. The numbers in the margin refer to relevant rules in section 11 of *Rules for Writers*, Seventh Edition. The first revision has been done for you.

What did Paul Revere do when he wasn't working for the Revolution? Quite apart from his famous ride, Paul Revere made other significant contributions to American life and culture.

The basic reason for all these contributions was ~~because~~ *that* Paul Revere was an   **11c**
enterprising entrepreneur. He originally followed his father into silversmithing. Soon after the war started, he began making gunpowder. He designed and printed paper money and made the state seal that Massachusetts still uses. By carving false teeth   **11a**
from rhinoceros tusks was one of his efforts to make money; publishing hymnbooks was another. He engraved copperplates for printing. He ran a hardware store and erected barns for local farmers.

Until Revere built the first rolling mill for copper in the United States, so all   **11a**
rolled copper had to be imported. He set up the equipment to cast bronze and made cannon for the army, copper fittings for the USS *Constitution* (Old Ironsides), and bells for churches. Seventy-five of his bells still ring from New England church steeples.

As a silversmith, a very creative field, Revere displayed great skill. His silver   **11b**
pieces were so beautifully crafted that two hundred years later one of his punch bowls brought an offer of a hundred thousand dollars. One reason that antique lovers today search for silver objects marked "Revere" is because Revere's work is so graceful.   **11c**
Modern artisans still try to duplicate his decorated grooves and flowing lines. And shoppers admire certain smoothly curved bowls are known as Revere bowls whether   **11a**
they are made of silver or of some other metal.

Whether or not he rode all the way to Concord, Paul Revere made an indelible impression on American life and culture.

Van Goor and Hacker, *Developmental Exercises for Rules for Writers*, 7th ed. (Boston: Bedford, 2012)

EXERCISE 12-1 ◆ Misplaced and dangling modifiers: Guided practice

Edit the following paragraphs to eliminate misplaced and dangling modifiers. The numbers in the margin refer to relevant rules in section 12 of *Rules for Writers*, Seventh Edition. The first revision has been done for you; a suggested revision of this exercise appears in the back of this book.

people usually think first of

Hearing the name Karl Marx, Russia. ~~is usually the first thought that comes to~~   12c

~~mind.~~ Marx never lived in Russia at all. Actually, he almost spent all of his adult life   12a

in England. He was a political exile for the last half of his life.

Marx lived first in Germany. Born of Jewish parents, his university studies   12e

were completed with a PhD at the University of Jena. His favorite professor tried to

get Marx an appointment to teach at the university. When that professor was fired,

Marx gave up hope of teaching at Jena or any other German university. Marx, because   12c

he was denied a university position, had to earn his living as a journalist. He worked

briefly as a newspaper editor in Germany.

Next came France, Belgium, and a return to Germany. First Marx and his new

bride moved to Paris, where Marx worked for a radical journal and became friendly

with Friedrich Engels. When the journal ceased publication, Marx moved to Brussels,

Belgium, and then back to Cologne, Germany. He did not hold a regular job, so he tried

desperately to at least earn enough money to feed his family.   12d

Marx decided after living in Paris and Brussels he would settle in London. He   12b

and his family lived in abject poverty while Marx earned what little income he could

by writing for an American newspaper, the *New York Tribune*.

EXERCISE 12-2 ♦ Misplaced modifiers

To read about this topic, see section 12 in *Rules for Writers*, Seventh Edition.

Circle the letter of the more effective sentence in each pair. Example:

    a. **Marx almost spent all his time writing, using every waking moment to get his ideas down on paper.**

    (b.) **Marx spent almost all his time writing, using every waking moment to get his ideas down on paper.**

1.   a.   Between 1852 and 1862, Marx just wrote more than three hundred articles for the *New York Tribune*.

    b.   Between 1852 and 1862, Marx wrote more than three hundred articles just for the *New York Tribune*.

2.   a.   During his lifetime, Marx did not receive much attention. But people all over the world paid attention to what he had written after his death.

    b.   During his lifetime, Marx did not receive much attention. But after his death, people all over the world paid attention to what he had written.

3.   a.   He wanted only one thing for himself: recognition of the importance of his ideas.

    b.   He only wanted one thing for himself: recognition of the importance of his ideas.

4.   a.   Capitalist scholars tend to usually say that Marx's work is "illogical" and "uninformed."

    b.   Capitalist scholars usually tend to say that Marx's work is "illogical" and "uninformed."

5.   a.   However, most capitalists agree that as a student of social organization he was brilliant.

    b.   However, most capitalists agree that he, as a student of social organization, was brilliant.

Van Goor and Hacker, *Developmental Exercises for Rules for Writers*, 7th ed. (Boston: Bedford, 2012)

EXERCISE 12-3 ◆ Misplaced and dangling modifiers

To read about this topic, see section 12 in *Rules for Writers*, Seventh Edition.

Circle the letter of the more effective sentence in each pair. Be prepared to explain your choice. Example:

    a. **Deciding that there were two classes of people in the world, they were named the "bourgeoisie" and the "proletariat."**

    (b.) **Deciding that there were two classes of people in the world, Marx named them the "bourgeoisie" and the "proletariat."**

1. a. Convinced that one major difference divided the people of the world into two groups, ownership of property was declared the basis for this division.

    b. Convinced that one major difference divided the people of the world into two groups, Marx declared that ownership of property was the basis for this division.

2. a. Marx defined anyone who owned property as bourgeois.

    b. Owning property of any kind, the property defined its owner as bourgeois.

3. a. Marx defined the proletariat as those who owned no property but labored to always produce wealth for the bourgeoisie.

    b. Marx defined the proletariat as those who owned no property but always labored to produce wealth for the bourgeoisie.

4. a. After finishing his study of economic history, Marx concluded that history is progressive and maybe even inevitable.

    b. Marx, after finishing his study of economic history, concluded that history is progressive and maybe even inevitable.

5. a. Denying God any role in human affairs, economic history was seen as a natural evolution in the world.

    b. Denying God any role in human affairs, Marx saw economic history as a natural evolution in the world.

Van Goor and Hacker, *Developmental Exercises for Rules for Writers*, 7th ed. (Boston: Bedford, 2012)

12-3 | Misplaced and dangling modifiers   **19**

EXERCISE 12-4 ◆ Misplaced and dangling modifiers: Guided review

Edit the following paragraphs to eliminate misplaced and dangling modifiers. The numbers in the margin refer to relevant rules in section 12 of *Rules for Writers*, Seventh Edition. The first revision has been done for you.

Marx wrote *The Communist Manifesto*, his most famous work, in collaboration with Friedrich Engels just before the German revolution of 1848. The book has three sections with distinct characteristics.

In the first section, Marx tries to ~~accurately~~ define terms^*accurately* and to state his basic

12d

assumptions. He traces the class systems of earlier times and concludes that there are only two classes in his day, the bourgeoisie and the proletariat. The bourgeoisie are the property-owning capitalists; the proletariat are the working class. Marx asserts that as the bourgeoisie increase their economic power, they work toward their own eventual downfall.

Set up in question-and-answer format, Marx made the second section of his

12e

Communist Manifesto resemble a debate with a bourgeois sympathizer. Of course, Marx only sees one side of the debate as being correct. After "defeating" his opponent

12a

on major questions, Marx presents his own ten-point program in clear, easy-to-understand, persuasive language.

Marx, after developing the second section in detail, moves on to the *Manifesto*'s

12c

final section. He shows how Communists and other reform groups work toward the same goals. Reminding workers that they "have nothing to lose but their chains," Marx calls on them to zealously and actively work together. Marx utters the slogan that can

12d

still be heard today in ringing tones: "Workers of the world, unite!"

12b

Van Goor and Hacker, *Developmental Exercises for Rules for Writers*, 7th ed. (Boston: Bedford, 2012)

EXERCISE 13-1 ◆ Distracting shifts: Guided practice

Edit the following paragraphs to eliminate distracting shifts. The numbers in the margin refer to relevant rules in section 13 of *Rules for Writers*, Seventh Edition. The first revision has been done for you; a suggested revision of this exercise appears in the back of this book.

it ended?

Do you know how slavery began in America or how ~~did it end~~? When the   13d

Mayflower landed in what is now Massachusetts in September 1620, slaves were

already in America. A Dutch ship had unloaded and sold twenty Africans in

Jamestown, Virginia, the year before.

Actually, slavery in America began long before that. Many early explorers

brought slaves with them to the new land, and some historians claim that one of the

men in Christopher Columbus's crew was a slave. From the 1500s to the 1800s, slave

ships brought ten million African slaves across the ocean.

Most of the slaves stayed in Latin America and the West Indies, but the

southern part of the United States received about 6 percent of them. Few northerners

owned slaves, and opposition to slavery was evident by the time of the American

Revolution. Rhode Island prohibited the importation of slaves even before the

Revolutionary War. After the war, six northern states abolish slavery at once,   13b

and other states pass laws to phase out slavery; even Virginia enacts legislation   13b

encouraging you to emancipate your slaves.   13a

But it took a war, a tricky political situation, and a very clever former slave

to free all slaves. History gives Abraham Lincoln the credit for liberating the slaves

during the Civil War, and he deserves some credit, but emancipation was not his idea.

Originally, no one in government seriously considered emancipation because they were   13a

so focused on winning the war to save the Union. Then an important black man talks   13b

to Lincoln and gives him the idea and the reason. This man said that freeing slaves

would be good for the war effort and would Lincoln agree to do it? Who was this man?   13d

He was Frederick Douglass, fugitive slave and newspaper editor.

Van Goor and Hacker, *Developmental Exercises for*
Rules for Writers, 7th ed. (Boston: Bedford, 2012)

13-1 | Distracting shifts: Guided practice   **21**

EXERCISE 13-2 ◆ Distracting shifts

To read about this topic, see section 13 in *Rules for Writers*, Seventh Edition.

A Edit the following sentences to eliminate distracting pronoun shifts. If a sentence is correct, mark it "OK." Example:

Frederick Douglass was born a slave, but he was lucky because his owner's wife did not

her

know that it was against the law for ~~you~~ to teach a slave to read and write.
                                       ^

1. A slave who learned to read and write gained self-confidence, so they were harder to oversee than illiterate slaves.

2. When he had learned enough to study on his own own, the slave Frederick Douglass did so; he used what he had learned to escape from his owner.

3. The master had told his slaves that all escape routes were blocked and that you would have no chance whatever at success.

4. Douglass used a simple but dangerous method of escape; he sailed from Baltimore to New York as a working sailor.

5. A listener could not learn anything about escape routes from Douglass's stories because Douglass told them nothing that would endanger other fugitives.

B Edit the following sentences to eliminate distracting shifts in verb tense. If a sentence is correct, mark it "OK." Example:

describes

Douglass's narrative tells about his own life as a child and ~~described~~ his torturous beatings
                                                              ^

by a professional "slave breaker."

6. Douglass had few ties to his mother and never meets his father.

7. Even when Douglass worked "out" for his master, his master got his wages.

8. His master sometimes allowed him to keep 1 percent (six cents out of six dollars); the master thought the money would encourage Douglass to work harder.

9. Douglass escapes by pretending to be someone else; he borrowed the identification papers of a freed black sailor.

10. Frederick Douglass used several different last names as he escaped slavery; an abolitionist friend suggests the name Douglass to him, and Frederick uses it from that time on.

Van Goor and Hacker, *Developmental Exercises for Rules for Writers*, 7th ed. (Boston: Bedford, 2012)

EXERCISE 13-3 ◆ Distracting shifts

To read about this topic, see section 13 in *Rules for Writers*, Seventh Edition.

Edit the following sentences to eliminate shifts between direct and indirect quotation or question. Example:

whether he

When Frederick was told to choose a new name, he asked could ~~he~~ keep Frederick and
^

take a new last name.

1. When a friend suggested Douglass as a last name, Frederick asked whether it was a satisfactory name and did it fit well with Frederick?

2. People frequently asked Douglass how did he feel when he found himself in a free state.

3. Lonely and frightened at the time, he said, "I can trust no man" and that he saw every white man as an enemy, every black man as a cause for distrust.

4. Douglass was befriended by David Ruggles, an abolitionist who asked him what did he plan to do.

5. Douglass married Anna and told her that they would move to New Bedford and don't worry because he would surely get a job there.

Van Goor and Hacker, *Developmental Exercises for Rules for Writers*, 7th ed. (Boston: Bedford, 2012)

13-3 | Distracting shifts   **23**

EXERCISE 13-4 ◆ Distracting shifts: Guided review

Edit the following paragraphs to eliminate any distracting shifts. The numbers in the margin refer to relevant rules in section 13 of *Rules for Writers*, Seventh Edition. The first revision has been done for you.

Frederick Douglass, who was born a slave and became a much-sought-after lecturer and writer, was a man of strong will and convictions.

Douglass never hesitated to defend the choices he ~~makes~~ *made* for himself and his   13b
family. On trains he sat in cars reserved for "whites only" until security officers
dragged him away. He walked out of a church when it was realized that none of his   13c
people could participate in the service until the white people were finished.

Wherever he lived, Douglass fought slavery. When he published his autobiography, *Narrative of the Life of Frederick Douglass*, in 1845, he was still a fugitive
slave. He and his wife moved to England the same year because he feared that his
book would reveal his identity as a fugitive slave. Also, some of his other writings had
aroused so much animosity that he fears for his life. From England, he wrote letters   13b
and worked to gain support for freeing the slaves. After friends in England raised
enough money to buy his freedom for him, he was even more determined to help
others gain their freedom. (Slaves used to say that a free black was never there when
you needed help, but no one could ever say that about Frederick Douglass.)   13a

Douglass was outspoken in his support for the causes he believed in. When the
Civil War broke out, Douglass comes back to the United States to help recruit African   13b
Americans to fight. "This war is for you and your children," he told them. Douglass
also supported woman suffrage, and he defended the right of members of different
races to marry if they wished. When Douglass married his second wife, a white
woman, critics complained. He answered them by saying, "My first wife was the color
of my mother" and that the second was the color of his father, so he was not playing   13d
favorites.

Van Goor and Hacker, *Developmental Exercises for Rules for Writers*, 7th ed. (Boston: Bedford, 2012)

EXERCISE 14-1 ◆ Emphasis: Guided practice

Edit the following paragraph to put major ideas in independent clauses and minor ideas in subordinate clauses or phrases. The numbers in the margin refer to relevant rules in section 14 of *Rules for Writers*, Seventh Edition. The first revision has been done for you; a suggested revision of this exercise appears in the back of this book.

No one who knew Albert Einstein as a young child would ever have believed that he might one day be called the smartest man in the world. None of his teachers could have predicted success for him. ~~Albert was a~~ slow learner. *A shy,* ~~He was shy. He~~ *Albert*   **14b** always got into trouble in class. He consistently failed some subjects. They were the   **14b** subjects he did not like. His family could not have predicted his success either. Albert could not even get to meals on time. Night after night his parents had to postpone dinner until servants searched the house and grounds and found the boy, at which   **14e** time he would be full of apologies but have no explanation to offer for his lateness except that he was "thinking." Once his angry father dangled his big gold watch at Albert. He told Albert to figure out how late he was. Albert, who was fascinated by   **14b, 14d** the tiny magnetic compass hanging from the watch chain, could not tell time. The boy asked so many questions about the compass that he did not eat much dinner anyway. Albert begged his father to lend him the compass to sleep with, and his father let him   **14c** borrow it. Years later Einstein wondered whether that little compass had been the beginning of his interest in science.

Van Goor and Hacker, *Developmental Exercises for Rules for Writers*, 7th ed. (Boston: Bedford, 2012)

14-1 | Emphasis: Guided practice   **25**

EXERCISE 14-2 ◆ Emphasis

To read about this topic, see section 14 in *Rules for Writers*, Seventh Edition.

Combine or restructure the following sentences so that the independent clause expresses the idea in brackets and everything else is subordinated. Example:

> who owned an electrochemical factory,
>
> **Albert Einstein's father, Hermann Einstein,** had some interest in science. ~~He owned an~~
>   ^
> ~~electrochemical factory.~~ **[Emphasize his father's interest in science.]**

1. Hermann Einstein moved his electrochemical business to Munich; the move made it possible for his son to have the best schooling available. [Emphasize the fact that Hermann moved his business.]

2. Albert Einstein's Uncle Jake explained math to the boy and made algebra problems into games. [Emphasize Uncle Jake's making games out of the problems.]

3. Albert's mother was impressed by her son's persistent questions and secretly hoped that Albert would one day be a professor. [Emphasize the mother's hope.]

4. One of Albert's friends was a medical student at the University of Munich. This friend supplied Albert with well-written modern books on natural science. [Emphasize that the friend supplied Einstein with books.]

5. Hermann Einstein kept his business in Munich for several years, and afterward he decided to go to Italy and work with relatives. [Emphasize the decision to go to Italy and work with relatives.]

Van Goor and Hacker, *Developmental Exercises for Rules for Writers*, 7th ed. (Boston: Bedford, 2012)

EXERCISE 14-3 ◆ Emphasis

To read about this topic, see section 14 in *Rules for Writers*, Seventh Edition.

Combine or restructure the following sentences so that the independent clause expresses the idea mentioned in brackets. Example:

> *When*
> **Hermann Einstein moved his family to Italy, ~~but~~ he left Albert in Munich to finish school.**
> ^
> **[Emphasize his leaving Albert in Munich to finish school.]**

1. Albert was miserably lonely without his family, and he had always depended on them for his social life. [Emphasize Albert's loneliness without his family.]

2. He did not get along with the other students. He did not get along with his teachers either. [Emphasize both ideas equally.]

3. He had never gotten along well with other students, and they envied his superior work in math and physics. [Emphasize his not getting along with other students.]

4. In mathematics he was smarter than his teachers, so his teachers resented him too. [Emphasize his teachers' resentment of him.]

5. He was desperate to be with his family in sunny Italy, so he faked a nervous breakdown. [Emphasize his faking a nervous breakdown.]

6. Albert convinced a medical doctor to sign a formal request for a six-month vacation, and then he found out that the school had expelled him. [Emphasize his discovery that the school had expelled him.]

7. His months in Italy were a welcome change, and they gave him time to enjoy life again and to plan for his future. [Emphasize that the months in Italy were a welcome change.]

8. Albert spent months thinking about his future while he enjoyed Italy's scenery, art, and music, and then he finally decided that he wanted to be a theoretical physicist. [Emphasize his decision to become a theoretical physicist.]

9. He knew that his father's business was not doing well, but he asked his father for enough money to take the entrance exams at the Swiss Federal Polytechnic School. [Emphasize his request to his father.]

10. His father wanted Albert to succeed, so he found the money somehow. [Emphasize his father's finding the money.]

EXERCISE 14-4 ◆ Emphasis: Guided review

Edit the following paragraph to put major ideas in independent clauses and minor ideas in subordinate clauses or phrases. The numbers in the margin refer to relevant rules in section 14 of *Rules for Writers*, Seventh Edition. The first revision has been done for you.

Teachers are not always right about their pupils. Certainly Albert Einstein's

teachers, ~~misjudged~~ *misjudging* his ability in math, ~~and they~~ failed to spot the most brilliant   14c

student they had ever had. Giuseppe Verdi's teachers made similar errors in judging

their pupil's musical ability. Verdi was Italian. He lived in the nineteenth century.   14b

He wanted to be a composer. He applied to the Conservatory of Music in Milan, and   14c

he was rejected because he "showed no aptitude for music." Today his works are

performed more than those of any other opera composer. Scientists have also been

underestimated. Everyone has heard of Charles Darwin, the British scientist. This

man, who also had trouble in school, was the first to propose the theory of evolution.   14d

He did so poorly at his school, which was the University of Edinburgh, that his   14e

teachers considered him hopeless, as a result of which they dismissed him. The first

American physicist to win the Nobel Prize for physics was also misjudged by his

teachers. Albert Abraham Michelson was a student at Annapolis. He was in the naval   14b

academy there. One of his teachers told him to pay less attention to science and

concentrate on naval gunnery. Luckily, Einstein, Verdi, Darwin, and Michelson refused

to accept their teachers' evaluations of them.

Van Goor and Hacker, *Developmental Exercises for Rules for Writers*, 7th ed. (Boston: Bedford, 2012)

EXERCISE 15-1 ◆ Variety: Guided practice

The following paragraphs are grammatically correct but dull. Revise them to add variety. You may need to combine some sentences. The numbers in the margin refer to relevant revision strategies in section 15 of *Rules for Writers*, Seventh Edition. The first revision has been done for you; a suggested revision of this exercise appears in the back of this book.

Everyone has heard of Martin Luther King Jr. *He studied* for the ministry at *After studying* Boston University and *earned* a doctorate in theology, *and then* he went home to the South to work as a minister. He started working in civil rights and became the most influential leader of that cause in America. When he died, the victim of an assassin's bullet, his name was almost synonymous with "civil rights." Historians and biographers have recorded his leadership in the fight to gain basic civil rights for all Americans. Many people who know of his civil rights work, however, are not aware of his skill as a writer. King produced other important writing in addition to his carefully crafted and emotional speeches.

15b, 15a
(See also 15c.)

15b

King's "Letter from Birmingham Jail" is among his most famous writings. He wrote it to answer a statement published by eight Alabama ministers that King's work was "unwise and untimely," and the letter shows King to be a man who had great patience with his critics. King is eager to get these ministers to accept his point of view, so he reminds them that they are ministers. Their goodwill, he says, should help them see that his views hold value. He does not attack them personally. He analyzes their arguments. Then he presents his own views. Does he use many of the emotional appeals for which he is justly famous? No, in this letter King depends on logic and reasoning as the tools to win his argument.

15c

15b, 15a
(See also 15c.)

15a
(See also 15c.)

15a
(See also 14b.)

Van Goor and Hacker, *Developmental Exercises for Rules for Writers*, 7th ed. (Boston: Bedford, 2012)

15-1 | Variety: Guided practice **29**

EXERCISE 15-2 ◆ Variety

To read about this topic, see section 15 in *Rules for Writers*, Seventh Edition.

Edit each of the following sentences in at least two ways, to provide varied openings and varied sentence structures. You may need to change other parts of each sentence as well. Example:

a. ~~Martin Luther King Jr. was in~~ *In* jail awaiting a hearing/, ~~he~~ *Martin Luther King Jr.* read a newspaper article attacking his work.

b. *When* Martin Luther King Jr. was in jail awaiting a hearing/, he read a newspaper article attacking his work.

1. a. King didn't have much to write on in the jail, so he started writing in the margins of the newspaper in which the article appeared.

    b. King didn't have much to write on in the jail, so he started writing in the margins of the newspaper in which the article appeared.

2. a. A black trusty, wanting to help King, was able to get some scraps of paper for him after a while.

    b. A black trusty, wanting to help King, was able to get some scraps of paper for him after a while.

3. a. His attorneys were later allowed to give him a pad of paper. King, fired up by the newspaper article, quickly filled the pad.

    b. His attorneys were later allowed to give him a pad of paper. King, fired up by the newspaper article, quickly filled the pad.

4. a. King chose to write his response to the newspaper article in letter form, so he seemed like the biblical Paul to some people.

    b. King chose to write his response to the newspaper article in letter form, so he seemed like the biblical Paul to some people.

5. a. How were King and Paul alike? Paul, a preacher of the Christian faith like King, wrote some of his famous letters from a prison cell.

    b. How were King and Paul alike? Paul, a preacher of the Christian faith like King, wrote some of his famous letters from a prison cell.

Van Goor and Hacker, *Developmental Exercises for Rules for Writers*, 7th ed. (Boston: Bedford, 2012)

EXERCISE 15-3 ◆ Variety: Guided review

The following paragraph is grammatically correct but dull. Revise it to add variety. You may need to combine some sentences. The numbers in the margin refer to relevant revision strategies in section 15 of *Rules for Writers*, Seventh Edition. The first revision has been done for you.

     Martin Luther King Jr.'s famous "Letter from Birmingham Jail" has a clearly

Beginning

thought-out structure. ~~King begins~~ with the statement that any nonviolent campaign

                                     --

has to go through four distinct stages./~~He says these stages are~~ fact finding,   15a or 15b

                                      --*King*

negotiation, self-purification, and direct action./~~He~~ says that he and his fellow

campaigners have gone through all these steps in Birmingham. King tries to reach his

readers after that beginning by asking them how to answer his children's questions   15a

about why they cannot go to the amusement park advertised on TV. The letter

discusses the difference between just and unjust laws, and it emphasizes the need for   15a or 15b

nonviolent direct action to dramatize the unjust ones. Next King mentions the "white   (See also 15c.)

moderates." He expresses his disappointment with white churches and white religious

leaders who have failed to join the civil rights movement, but he praises the few who

have helped. He describes the mistreatment he and his friends have suffered at the   15a or 15b

hands of the local police, and he gives thanks for the courage of the people involved in   (See also 15c.)

sit-ins and bus strikes. King writes finally of his faith that the movement will survive   15b

and prosper and that racial prejudice will soon pass away.

Van Goor and Hacker, *Developmental Exercises for Rules for Writers*, 7th ed. (Boston: Bedford, 2012)

15-3 | Variety: Guided review   **31**

REVIEW OF 8–15 ◆ Clarity (effective sentences)

Edit the following paragraphs to eliminate sentence problems. Section numbers in the margin refer to suggested revision strategies in *Rules for Writers*, Seventh Edition. The first revision has been done for you.

One of the men who greatly influenced Martin Luther King Jr. was Mahatma

Gandhi, ~~and he~~ *who* introduced nonviolent protest techniques in Africa and India. Gandhi   14c

is called the father of his country, and he helped India gain its freedom from England.   14c

Gandhi's nonviolent method was based on three principles: courage, being truthful,

and you had to have endurance. By using nonviolent techniques is how Gandhi helped   9a, 11a

Indians in Africa and India.

After studying law in London, he attempts to practice law in India but is   13b

not very successful. When he went to South Africa to do legal work in 1893, he was

abused because he was an Indian who also claimed the rights of a British subject.

Although he had planned to stay in Africa one year, he remained for twenty-one years.

Fighting injustice in South Africa, the principle of *satyagraha* (nonviolent protest) was   12e

developed by Gandhi during those years.   8a

After working in South Africa, Gandhi returned to India to lead the Indian

movement for independence. While in India, he led hundreds of his followers on a

march to the sea. There they made salt from seawater to protest a law. That law   14b

required them to buy all their salt from the government. He also began programs of

hand weaving and spinning among the poor that exist to this day.   12b

Although Gandhi believed and lived by the nonviolent principle of *satyagraha*,   10a

he died a violent death. In 1948, he was assassinated by a high-caste Hindu fanatic.

This man feared Gandhi's tolerance for all creeds and religions. Nevertheless,   14b

Gandhi's nonviolent methods have survived to this day. When Martin Luther King

Jr. began his civil rights work in the United States, many people compared him to

Gandhi, saying that his principles were essentially the same as Gandhi.   10c

Van Goor and Hacker, *Developmental Exercises for Rules for Writers*, 7th ed. (Boston: Bedford, 2012)

EXERCISE 16-1 ◆ Wordy sentences: Guided practice

Edit the following paragraph to make any wordy sentences as short as possible without changing their meaning. The numbers in the margin refer to relevant rules in section 16 of *Rules for Writers*, Seventh Edition. The first two revisions have been done for you; a suggested revision of this exercise appears in the back of this book.

Adam Smith, the founder of modern economics, proposed a theory in the
eighteenth century that has made him controversial ever since. This ~~British~~   16a
economist, ~~who was~~ born in Scotland and educated in England, wrote the first   16e
complete study of political economy. *The Wealth of Nations* was published in the same
year that Americans declared their independence from England—that was in 1776.   16e
Smith's book pointed out and directed attention to the interdependence of freedom and   16a
order, economic processes, and free-trade laws. Although Smith's thinking did not
really affect economic policies significantly during his lifetime, its influence in the
next century was considerable. Among economists, the phrases "the invisible hand"
and "laissez-faire" are synonymous with Smith's name. History has only made Smith's
ideas more controversial. Say "Adam Smith" to conservative businesspeople, and those   16b
same people will smile and make a response with words like "He was a good man—   16d
really understood how business works!" Say "Adam Smith" to liberal reformers, and
they will grimace and mutter something along the lines of "He was an evil man—   16c
really sold the average citizen down the river." Both of these reactions are extreme,
but such responses indicate that the controversy aroused by Smith's ideas is still alive.

Van Goor and Hacker, *Developmental Exercises for
Rules for Writers*, 7th ed. (Boston: Bedford, 2012)

16-1 | Wordy sentences: Guided practice   **33**

EXERCISE 16-2 ◆ Wordy sentences

To read about this topic, see section 16 in *Rules for Writers*, Seventh Edition.

Tighten the following sentences by eliminating redundancies, unnecessary repetition, and empty phrases. The number in parentheses at the end of each sentence is a suggested maximum number of words for your revised sentence. Example:

> ~~It is a fact that~~ Adam Smith wanted to find a theory ~~that would~~ ^to^ explain how the economic world functions. (14)

1. It seems that after many years of study and then years of writing, he published a book that was called *The Wealth of Nations*. (14)

2. This lengthy, protracted book had in the neighborhood of a thousand pages, and those pages included a sixty-three-page index. (12)

3. The full and complete title of his book indicates the comprehensive, all-inclusive scope of the book: *An Inquiry into the Nature and Causes of the Wealth of Nations*. (19. Do not shorten the twelve-word title.)

4. Smith believed that there are certain basic, essential economic laws in existence and that these laws work to the benefit of everyone if people "let the market alone." (17)

5. He believed that something along the lines of an "invisible hand" guides economics. (10)

Van Goor and Hacker, *Developmental Exercises for Rules for Writers*, 7th ed. (Boston: Bedford, 2012)

EXERCISE 16-3 ◆ Wordy sentences

To read about this topic, see section 16 in *Rules for Writers*, Seventh Edition.

Tighten the following sentences without changing their meaning. The number in parentheses at the end of each sentence is a suggested maximum number of words for your revised sentence. Example:

> *if*
> **Adam Smith saw the market as ~~something that is~~ "self-regulating" ~~as long as~~ everyone**
> ^
> **leaves it alone. (12)**

1. Adam Smith said that there are two laws that govern the field of economics. (8)

2. The first basic, important, essential law that governs the field of economics is self-interest. (5, but can you do it in 3?)

3. The one who is employed wants a higher wage; the one who employs the worker wants a higher profit. (12)

4. The second law, which is the law of competition, works only if there is no manipulation of the market by anyone. (12)

5. Because people will buy the gloves that cost the least, a manufacturer of gloves cannot raise prices for gloves too much without bringing about the result that people who buy gloves go to competitors who sell gloves for a lower price. (25)

6. The term that has been given to Smith's "let the market alone" policy by economists is "laissez-faire." (9)

7. Adam Smith urged governments to practice the policy of laissez-faire with the resulting effect that it would allow "the invisible hand" to regulate the marketplace. (16)

8. Smith assumed that there was a "law of accumulation" that works by requiring industrialists to add buildings and machinery, to hire more workers, and to produce more goods. (23)

9. There was another law that he called the "law of population" that supplies the workers that are necessary. (10)

10. In the long run, said Smith, those who do the work will be paid, the industrialists who employ those who do the work will make a fair profit, and the landlords who rent space to the industrialists will have many tenants. (21)

Van Goor and Hacker, *Developmental Exercises for Rules for Writers*, 7th ed. (Boston: Bedford, 2012)

16-3 | Wordy sentences **35**

EXERCISE 16-4 ◆ Wordy sentences: Guided review

Edit the following paragraph to make any wordy sentences as short as possible without changing their meaning. The numbers in the margin refer to relevant rules in section 16 of *Rules for Writers*, Seventh Edition. The first wordy sentence has been revised for you.

Adam Smith was convinced ~~in his mind~~ that if people would "let the market   16a

alone," all would be well. The true facts about how the market operated during the   16a

next century would have distressed him. The industrialists chose Smith as the patron

saint for industrialists. Working to make sure that the government "let the market   16b

alone," they opposed even laws that forbade shackling children to the machines that

were operated by them. By means of agreements that were secret, they agreed to   16d, 16e

charge identical prices. Similarly, workers agreed to demand the same wages from

every employer. Neither employers nor employees followed Adam Smith's injunction

to let the market alone. It seems quite obvious that there can be no doubt that Adam   16c

Smith would be disappointed in the way his economic theories have been used—and

misused.

Van Goor and Hacker, *Developmental Exercises for Rules for Writers*, 7th ed. (Boston: Bedford, 2012)

EXERCISE 17-1 ◆ Appropriate language: Guided practice

A The writer of the following paragraph used language that is too informal for the audience—an educated group of nonexperts. Revise the paragraph by replacing slang, regional expressions, nonstandard English, and sexist language. The numbers in the margin refer to relevant rules in section 17 of *Rules for Writers*, Seventh Edition. The first revision has been done for you; a suggested revision of this exercise appears in the back of this book.

                            Englishman

In the 1800s, an ~~English dude~~ named Thomas Robert Malthus became involved   17c

in economics. He was really psyched about predicting how many more people would   17c

populate the world eventually and how much food would be available for them. What

he figured out was gross. He said that people kept having children faster than men   17c, 17d

could produce enough to feed them. There was no way to avoid it. Hard times and wars

would do most people in. According to Malthus, famine, plagues, and even wars were   17c

necessary to knock off some excess people so the remainder could have enough food.   17c

B The writer of the following paragraph used too much puffed-up language for an audience of educated nonexperts. Revise the paragraph, replacing jargon, pretentious language, and sexist language. Numbers in the margin refer to relevant rules in section 17 of *Rules for Writers*, Seventh Edition. The first revision has been done for you; a suggested revision of this exercise appears in the back of this book.

                            population grows faster than food supplies.

Robert Malthus proved that ~~the progression of population is exponential while~~   17b

~~the amplification of foodstuffs proceeds mathematically.~~ His cerebrations led him to   17b

oppose any help for economically deprived people. He believed that by relieving the   17b

immediate problems of the poor, the government actually made it harder for everyone

to feed his family. Malthus said that if the government subsidized their basic needs,   17e

people would only have more children, thus increasing the population even more.

Then the inevitable famine or drought would have to eliminate even more people to

facilitate the survival of a few. Everyone from worker to foreman was caught in the   17a, 17e

same predicament. It is no wonder that when the English historian Thomas Carlyle

finished reading Malthus's theories, he pronounced economics "the dismal science."

EXERCISE 17-2 ◆ Appropriate language

To read about this topic, see section 17 in *Rules for Writers*, Seventh Edition.

Change the italicized words and phrases in the following sentences to more appropriate language for an educated audience of nonexperts. Consult the dictionary if necessary. Do not change the meaning of any sentence. Example:

> **David Ricardo was another nineteenth-century economist who thought people *~~had to stay~~* ^{could not}**
>
> *improve their social position.*
> *~~put in their social class.~~*

1. Ricardo and Malthus were *tight, close buddies*, but they argued constantly.

2. They did agree on one thing: The future looked *inauspicious* for humanity.

3. Ricardo didn't *figure it all out* just by calculating population growth.

4. He accumulated statistical *corroboration* for the validity of his theory of economics.

5. His theory predicted that workers would always be *lowest on the totem pole*, that industrialists would barely be able to *hang in there*, and that landowners would always be wealthy and powerful.

6. His theory made the landowners the *bad guys*.

7. In those days, landowners were called "landlords"; they rented land to tenant *agriculturists*.

8. Landlords collected rents; but since their land also supplied food for the country, they held *humongous* power.

9. Landlords would *as lief* die as give up their power.

10. When landlords *upped* land-rent fees, workers had to pay more for bread and the industrialists had to pay higher wages without getting any increase in production.

Van Goor and Hacker, *Developmental Exercises for Rules for Writers*, 7th ed. (Boston: Bedford, 2012)

EXERCISE 17-3 ◆ Appropriate language

To read about this topic, see section 17 in *Rules for Writers*, Seventh Edition.

Circle the letter of the more appropriately worded sentence in each pair. Assume an educated audience of nonexperts, and be prepared to explain your choices. Example:

a. **Malthus did not come up with any suggestions for ameliorating the lot of the common man.**

(b.) **Malthus did not suggest any way to make life better for ordinary people.**

1. a. Malthus opposed loans to the poor because he did not believe poor families would ever have enough income to deal with negative savings.

   b. Malthus opposed loans to the poor because he saw no way for poor people to increase their income enough to pay off debts.

2. a. Every member of society found that his life was impacted by Malthus's "laws" and their parameters.

   b. No one escaped the consequences of Malthus's "laws": Rich and poor both suffered the consequences of overpopulation.

3. a. Malthus saw hope only in limiting marriages; he believed that if marriages were restrained, there would be fewer eventual workers and wages would go up.

   b. The one bright idea Malthus had was to put a brake on marriages; fewer weddings meant fewer kids and eventually fewer workers and higher wages.

4. a. Ricardo said that the value added to a product by a man's labor was often greater than the wages paid to the laborer.

   b. Ricardo said that the value workers added to a product was not reflected in the workers' wages.

5. a. In Ricardo's view, there was no viable system workers could utilize to improve their lot; they would always be stuck between a rock and a hard place.

   b. Ricardo said that workers had almost no hope of improving their lives.

Van Goor and Hacker, *Developmental Exercises for Rules for Writers*, 7th ed. (Boston: Bedford, 2012)

17-3 | Appropriate language   **39**

Name _____ Section _____ Date _____

EXERCISE 17-4 ◆ Appropriate language: Guided review

Revise the following paragraph using standard English free of slang, jargon, pretentious language, and sexist language. The numbers in the margin refer to relevant rules in section 17 of *Rules for Writers*, Seventh Edition. The first sentence has been revised for you.

                   The

~~The relation between the~~ theories of economists Thomas Malthus and David

    show certain similarities,^but one theory did not lead to the other.

Ricardo ~~is associative rather than causal.~~ Their visions of the future are similar,   **17a**

but each arrived at his conclusions on his own. Ricardo predicted a dreary future;

he said that future workers would not have enough moolah to buy bread. It was   **17c**

not exactly the same picture Malthus painted, but it was equally dismal. A modern

scholar, Robert Heilbroner, once said that these two men "changed the world from

an optimistic to a pessimistic one." Before them, most people believed that the world

would just naturally get sweeter. After them, the natural world seemed to be an   **17c**

enemy of the world's people. Although both Malthus and Ricardo studied the problem,

neither of them could render intelligible the reasons for the recurring fluctuations   **17b**

in the country's economic well-being. Nor could any other economist who offered his   **17e**

theories on the subject. Malthus and Ricardo saw only a gloomy image of future life.

Scrupulously honest, they reported that vision but offered no solutions to the problems

they predicted. For many people, economics continues to be a dismal attempt to

elucidate the reasons for the behavior of phenomena in the market.   **17b**

Van Goor and Hacker, *Developmental Exercises for Rules for Writers,* 7th ed. (Boston: Bedford, 2012)

EXERCISE 18-1 ◆ Exact words: Guided practice

In the following paragraph, replace general words with specific ones and revise clichés and mixed figures of speech. Be sure that connotations are appropriate, that idioms are used properly, and that words are not misused. The numbers in the margin refer to relevant rules in section 18 of *Rules for Writers*, Seventh Edition. The first revision has been done for you; a suggested revision of this exercise appears in the back of this book.

                                 dominated

Economics is not totally ~~domineered~~ by men. Even in the 1800s, when Thomas   **18c**

Malthus and David Ricardo were the experts, one leading writer about economics was

a woman, Jane Marcet. Marcet wrote for the popular press. One of her favorite things   **18b**

to write about was political economy. In her book *Conversations in Political Economy*,

Marcet summarized economic doctrines before 1800. Her aim was different than that   **18d**

of either Malthus or Ricardo. Rather than propounding a new theory of her own, she

was happy as a lark to popularize theories of other people. Modern-day women have   **18e**

done more than write about theories that men have proposed. Some of them have

taken the bull by the horns and charged full steam ahead. Carmen M. Reinhart, for   **18f**

example, has written influential papers on financial crises and has served in high-

level positions in research and government organizations. She is just one of the

increasing number of ladies making careers in economics.   **18a**

EXERCISE 18-2 ◆ Exact words

To read about this topic, see section 18 in *Rules for Writers*, Seventh Edition.

A In each of the following sentences, circle the more specific word or phrase in parentheses. Example:

Alice Mitchell Rivlin was an important (person /(economist)) in the federal government.

1. Rivlin worked for (an important government office / the US Congressional Budget Office), where she (secured an important position / became director of that office).

2. She received her BA from (Bryn Mawr College / a prestigious eastern women's college) and her (PhD / highest degree) from Radcliffe College.

3. Rivlin's first job, at (the Brookings Institution / a think tank) in Washington, DC, lasted (for some time / from 1957 to 1966).

4. Most of her (publications / books) have been (put out / published) by the Brookings Institution.

5. Rivlin's interest in government finances carried over into the educational world when she became (a teacher / a professor of public policy) at (George Mason University near Washington, DC / a university in northern Virginia).

B Edit the following sentences to replace words with inappropriate connotations. (See a thesaurus, the glossary of usage [p. 653] in *Rules for Writers*, Seventh Edition, or a dictionary if necessary.) Example:

         perceptive

Alice Rivlin was ~~crafty~~ enough to understand the interrelatedness of individual budget items.

6. She planned to execute a thorough analysis of every part of the federal budget.

7. Rivlin did not claim that federal government services were cheap.

8. What she pushed was the idea that legislators should have easy access to information they needed.

9. She allowed herself no alibi for incomplete work.

10. Rivlin's work has proved conclusively that ladies can be extremely competent in financial matters.

Van Goor and Hacker, *Developmental Exercises for Rules for Writers*, 7th ed. (Boston: Bedford, 2012)

EXERCISE 18-3 ◆ Exact words

To read about this topic, see section 18 in *Rules for Writers*, Seventh Edition.

A Circle the correct word or expression in parentheses. Example:

Alice Rivlin had the skill and (patients /(patience)) to analyze the federal budget; she (planned on doing /(planned to do)) a thorough job.

1. She wanted her work to have one specific (effect / affect), and she was determined to (try and / try to) succeed.

2. She planned (on making / to make) the budget, that (incredible / incredulous) mass of material, more available to Congress before Congress actually needed it.

3. She had no (allusions / illusions) about the difficulty of the task; luckily for Congress, she proved (capable to do / capable of doing) it.

4. When voting on the budget becomes (eminent / imminent / immanent), members of Congress need some (type of a / type of) clear, easy-to-understand document.

5. That document must be easily (assessable / accessible) to any representatives who (plan on voting / plan to vote).

B Edit the following sentences to correct any misused words or idioms. Mark the one correct sentence "OK." (See 18c, 18d, the glossary of usage [p. 653] in *Rules for Writers*, Seventh Edition, or a dictionary if necessary.) Example:

                                       complement

The work of the Congressional Budget Office should ~~compliment~~ the work of Congress.

6. Members of Congress have been known to get very angry at a budget director whose work was not satisfactory.

7. Sometimes the Budget Office must try and please a representative.

8. The director of the Budget Office, however, must maintain that office's independents from members of Congress.

9. Perhaps Alice Rivlin's style was different than that of some other budget officers, for she got the job done without making too many enemies.

10. In fact, Rivlin's performance at the Budget Office may account for her becoming director of the Office of Management and Budget in 1994.

Van Goor and Hacker, *Developmental Exercises for Rules for Writers*, 7th ed. (Boston: Bedford, 2012)

18-3 | Exact words **43**

EXERCISE 18-4 ◆ Exact words

To read about this topic, see section 18 in *Rules for Writers*, Seventh Edition.

Edit the following sentences to eliminate or replace clichés and to clarify mixed figures of speech. Mark the two correct sentences "OK." Example:

> *be undertaking too much*
> Would an economist ~~bite off more than she could chew~~ if she tried to find out why better
>   ^
> *fail to materialize?*
> financial rewards for women so often ~~hang fire?~~
>   ^

1. Rivlin has had more than one iron in the fire; besides her budget work, she has written several books and taught public policy at George Mason University.

2. Rivlin did not sweep problems under the rug to take root there and come unraveled; she dealt with them before they became bigger problems.

3. When Rivlin received a MacArthur Foundation award, it was crystal clear that her talents and dedication had been recognized.

4. Rivlin is not the only modern woman to choose economics for her specialty.

5. Looking for such women is no longer like hunting for a needle in a haystack.

6. It goes without saying that women's roles in the labor market have changed radically.

7. It is a crying shame that the economic status of women has not kept pace with these changes. Why?

8. She may have been playing with fire, but Cynthia Lloyd wanted to get her feet wet dealing with that question.

9. In so doing, she made the study of women in the labor market an integral and accepted part of economic analysis.

10. Her studies don't claim that money grows on trees but ask why women's efforts to get their share are always put on the back burner.

Van Goor and Hacker, *Developmental Exercises for Rules for Writers*, 7th ed. (Boston: Bedford, 2012)

EXERCISE 18-5 ◆ Exact words: Guided review

Edit the following paragraph for language appropriate for an audience of educated nonexperts. The numbers in the margin refer to relevant rules in section 18 of *Rules for Writers*, Seventh Edition. The first revision has been done for you; find and correct the other five problems.

                                   from

    Women economists have been no different ~~than~~ men economists in the range of   18d

their interests. Jane Marcet was interested in writing about economics for the popular

press, not in developing theories of her own. Jane Jacobs concentrated on cities

because she believed that they have a significance impact on national economies.   18c

She claimed that only cities can maintain or effect a nation's economic life enough to   18c

cause real change. Phyllis Deane studied developing countries. She kept her shoulder   18e

to the wheel to find ways to try and understand the economies of these countries.   18d

Cynthia Lloyd's primary concern is for improved economic status for women in the

labor market. Alice Rivlin stays busy as a bee from her association with the Brookings   18e

Institution in Washington, DC, and with financial boards and organizations.

REVIEW OF 16–18 ◆ Clarity (word choice)

Edit the following essay to eliminate problems with word choice. The numbers in the margin refer to relevant rules in sections 16–18 of *Rules for Writers*, Seventh Edition. The first revision has been done for you.

Economics, ~~which is~~ a branch of social science, deals with the production,   16e

distribution, and consumption of goods and services. However, you'd better believe it's   17c

not an exact science, though economists strive to make it so.

Economists have several aggravating habits. One of the worst is the habit of   18c

"two-handedness." An economist will say, "On the one hand, interest rates may rise

and . . ." In the next breath, he will say, "On the other hand, interest rates may fall   17e

and . . ." President Harry Truman used to get angry at advisers who talked like that.   18c

He once said that what he really needed was a one-handed economist.

If the current volume of *Who's Who in Economics* fell off of its library shelf,   18d

the floor would be dented by this thousand-page book. Hundreds of names are in

that volume, but the same few keep rising to the top and surfacing. Whenever people   16b

discuss economics, they nearly always refer to Malthus, Ricardo, Veblen, or last but   18e

not least Keynes. But the same name nearly always heads the list. Just as cream   18f

always rises to the top of the ladder of success, Adam Smith's name has led all the rest

for more than two centuries.

Pretend you are the host of a current TV show about money. Pretend also that

you write books with titles like *The Money Game* and *Supermoney*. What type of a   18d

name would you choose for your *nom de plume*? You would want an easily recognized   17b

name. You might do just what George Jerome W. Goodman did when he started a

successful TV show about managing money: He called himself "Adam Smith."

Van Goor and Hacker, *Developmental Exercises for Rules for Writers*, 7th ed. (Boston: Bedford, 2012)

EXERCISE 19-1 ◆ Fragments: Guided practice

Edit the following paragraphs to eliminate sentence fragments. The numbers in the margin refer to relevant rules in section 19 of *Rules for Writers*, Seventh Edition. The first revision has been done for you; a suggested revision of this exercise appears in the back of this book.

                                                                                      Four
~~How four~~ young Englishmen added a word to the world's vocabulary in the   19a
                      ^

1960s. A word that became synonymous with the 1960s. Especially with the music of   19b, 19c

that time. That word was, of course, "Beatles." The Beatles became the most famous

popular musical group of the twentieth century. And have held the loyalty of many   19c

fans into the present century.

    The Beatles were popular in Liverpool, England, and in Hamburg, Germany.

Before they came to America on tour and became world famous. Liverpool and   19a

Hamburg loved the four young men and their music. The Beatles' favorite club was

the Cavern in Liverpool. Where they hung out together, played day and night, and   19a

attracted many fans. A Liverpool disc jockey first called attention to them, and a

Liverpool music critic and record store owner became their first manager. The disc

jockey called them "fantastic." Saying that they had "resurrected original rock 'n'   19b

roll." The music critic who became their manager, Brian Epstein, made them shape

up as a group. Promoting them, arranging club dates for them, and badgering record   19b

companies for them. He was determined to win a recording contract for this exciting

new group.

    In England, the record buying led to the publicity. In America, the publicity led

to the record buying. Everyone wanted copies of the original singles. "Love Me Do,"   19c

"Please, Please Me," and "From Me to You." In America, audiences made so much noise

that no one could hear the music. Crowds of screaming teenagers surrounded the

Beatles wherever they went. Determined to touch one or more of these famous music   19b

makers. Reporters observing the conduct of fans at Beatles' concerts found that they

had to invent a new word. To describe the wild, almost insane behavior of the fans.   19b

They called it "Beatlemania."

Van Goor and Hacker, *Developmental Exercises for*
Rules for Writers, 7th ed. (Boston: Bedford, 2012)

19-1 | Fragments: Guided practice   **47**

EXERCISE 19-2 ◆ Fragments

To read about this topic, see section 19 in *Rules for Writers*, Seventh Edition.

Each of the following word groups includes a subordinating word. One word group in each pair contains a fragment. Write "OK" after each item that does not contain a fragment and write "frag" after each item that contains a fragment. Example:

    a. **John Lennon lived with his Aunt Mimi until he was grown. Because his parents had separated and his mother had given John to Mimi.** *frag*

    b. **His father took him from Mimi when John was about five. Because his mother returned him to Mimi, he grew up as Mimi's child.** *OK*

1. a.   When John Lennon was a teenager, his mother, Julia, began to pay more attention to his interests.

   b.   When Julia, John Lennon's mother, bought him a guitar and let him stay with her instead of his Aunt Mimi.

2. a.   Although he studied art in college, he soon became more interested in music.

   b.   Although Julia encouraged his music and put up with the boyish pranks that annoyed Aunt Mimi.

3. a.   His mother died before he was an adult. While John was still in college, in fact.

   b.   Mimi's husband, his uncle, had died while John still lived with them.

4. a.   John asked Paul McCartney to join his group, and later Paul brought in George Harrison, and all three asked Ringo Starr to join them. Before they cut their first record.

   b.   In their early days, the Beatles copied people like Elvis Presley and Little Richard. Before these English boys even visited America, they sang with American accents.

5. a.   The Beatles gave one reason for quitting their tours in 1966. That the tours were wrecking their playing.

   b.   Stopping the tours gave the Beatles an opportunity to expand their talents. That they learned to read musical notes and write their own music was key to their improvement as musicians.

Van Goor and Hacker, *Developmental Exercises for Rules for Writers*, 7th ed. (Boston: Bedford, 2012)

EXERCISE 19-3 ◆ Fragments

To read about this topic, see section 19 in *Rules for Writers*, Seventh Edition.

Underline each fragment in the following paragraphs. (Consult the chart on p. 181 of *Rules for Writers*, Seventh Edition, if necessary.) Do not correct the errors, but be prepared to discuss possible revision strategies for each fragment. The first fragment is underlined for you.

Paul McCartney wrote many of the Beatles' songs. A good student who learned quickly, he began composing songs when he was about fourteen.

Paul said that sometimes a song just came to him, like "Eleanor Rigby." <u>One of his most famous and moving songs.</u> The song is about a lonely woman who can't connect with other people. Paul was sitting at the piano not working on anything special. Just fooling around with melodies and rhythms. Then some notes played themselves in his head, and so did some words. Like "Daisy Hawkins picks up the rice in the church where a wedding has been." Later Paul saw the name "Rigby" on a shop in Bristol. And decided he liked that name better than "Hawkins," especially with "Eleanor" instead of "Daisy." He and John Lennon finished the song together.

Paul wrote "Hey, Jude" in an effort to help John's son, Julian, who was upset over his parents' separation. Paul wanted the boy not to be sad. "To take a sad song and make it better." He decided to change "Julian" to "Jude" after he finished the song. Because he wanted the song to have a country-and-western feel.

All of the Beatles wrote songs, and often they collaborated on one, but Paul McCartney and John Lennon wrote most of the songs the Beatles sang.

Van Goor and Hacker, *Developmental Exercises for Rules for Writers*, 7th ed. (Boston: Bedford, 2012)

19-3 | Fragments   **49**

EXERCISE 19-4 ◆ Fragments

To read about this topic, see section 19 in *Rules for Writers*, Seventh Edition.

Correct the fragments in the following paragraphs. The first revision has been done for you. Find and revise ten more fragments.

George Harrison was known in school for two things/, ~~His~~ *his* sharp clothes and his love of the guitar. His mother said he sometimes practiced the guitar for hours. Not stopping until his fingers were bleeding. When George met John Lennon, he found another guitar lover. Although they went to the same school, they did not meet there. Because George was two years younger and they had no classes together. Instead, they met on the school bus. After they became friends, they spent most of their time at George's house, playing their guitars.

When George, John, Paul McCartney, and Ringo Starr formed a group, the four experimented with all kinds of things. From melodies and sounds to drugs. George, however, began to want more out of life. To find answers to the big questions he had about war and loneliness and reasons for living. The others agreed to search with him, and George Harrison became their guide.

Later, George and his wife went to India. Where a religious festival they attended impressed them deeply. When George returned to England, he read many books about meditation. And went to hear Indian holy teachers. He shared what he read and heard with the other Beatles. Who were just as interested as George was. When George learned that a holy man called the Maharishi was going to speak on transcendental meditation, he told his friends. They all went to listen to him. To learn whatever they could that would help them.

The Beatles were headed in a new direction. A direction that was obvious in their next album, *Sgt. Pepper's Lonely Hearts Club Band*. The album had innovative lyrics and an amazing musical background. A forty-one-piece orchestra, guitar, sitar, doubled voices, a comb-and-paper instrument, and all kinds of electronic and percussion tricks. The Beatles were no longer copycat rock 'n' rollers.

Van Goor and Hacker, *Developmental Exercises for Rules for Writers*, 7th ed. (Boston: Bedford, 2012)

EXERCISE 19-5 ◆ Fragments

To read about this topic, see section 19 in *Rules for Writers*, Seventh Edition.

Half of the following word groups are complete sentences. The other half contain fragments. Correct the fragments, and mark the complete sentences "OK." Example:

> *because*
> **As a child and a teenager, Ringo Starr spent a total of three years in the hospital/~~Because~~**
> **of two severe health problems.**

1. When Ringo Starr was six, a burst appendix put him in the hospital for a whole year. Because of problems the rupture caused.

2. His doctors had to perform several operations; Ringo could not attend school at all that year.

3. His babysitter taught him to read and write, so he did not fall too far behind in his schoolwork.

4. When he was thirteen, Ringo had to go back into the hospital. And stay there for two years while doctors treated a lung condition.

5. At age fifteen, he worked at various jobs. But what he really liked best was playing the drums for his many fans.

6. Having taught himself on drums he bought on the installment plan, he played with different musical groups in Liverpool, including the Beatles.

7. When Ringo joined the Beatles, not everyone was sure that he could handle the job. For example, George Martin, a record producer who invited them to London to record an album.

8. Martin insisted on a standby drummer as insurance. Someone ready to step in just in case Ringo was not good enough.

9. Ringo's many devoted fans were not surprised when he handled the job and became a full-fledged Beatle, making new friends at every engagement.

10. Many people considered him the most likable member of the group. Because of his easy smile and his open approach to life.

Van Goor and Hacker, *Developmental Exercises for Rules for Writers*, 7th ed. (Boston: Bedford, 2012)

19-5 | Fragments **51**

EXERCISE 19-6 ◆ Fragments: Guided review

Find and correct the sentence fragments in the following paragraphs. The numbers in the margin refer to relevant rules in section 19 of *Rules for Writers*, Seventh Edition. The first revision has been done for you.

Many people influenced the Beatles in their career. For example, Bob Waller, a disc jockey in Liverpool,/, ~~He~~ first called attention to them in one of his articles. "They resurrected original rock 'n' roll," he wrote. When he first heard them in 1961. From Stu Sutcliffe, a talented musician who sometimes played with them, the Beatles copied several things. Their hairstyle, their dress, and much of their philosophy. George Martin, who produced their records, advised them how to improve after their early records. And taught them how to use tapes.

    19c
    19a
    19c
    19c

The person who influenced them most, however, was Brian Epstein. Owner of several record stores and reviewer of new records. When a customer asked for a record by a group Epstein had never heard of, he went from club to club. Looking for a group calling itself "The Beatles." By the end of 1961, he had become the group's manager. Convinced that he had found talented and original musicians. His contract said that he was to promote the Beatles and arrange their tours and club dates. His other duty was really the most important. To get record contracts for them.

    19b
    19b
    19b
    19b

Epstein did far more than his contract called for. He made the young men wear suits every time they performed. Until their gray, collarless outfits became a symbol of the Beatles. He made another demand of them. That they be on time for appearances. He even made them quit chewing gum onstage. And by the time he had done all these things, he had also gotten them a recording date. Why were the Beatles so devastated by Epstein's death? When Brian Epstein was found dead of an accidental drug overdose in 1967. The Beatles lost far more than a good manager. They lost a close friend and mentor.

    19a
    19a
    19a

Van Goor and Hacker, *Developmental Exercises for Rules for Writers*, 7th ed. (Boston: Bedford, 2012)

EXERCISE 20-1 ◆ Run-on sentences: Guided practice

Edit the following paragraphs to eliminate run-on sentences. Each rule number in the margin indicates a problem and suggests an effective method of revision. See section 20 of *Rules for Writers*, Seventh Edition. The first revision has been done for you; a suggested revision of this exercise appears in the back of this book.

Not

Have you ever heard of the Wobblies./? ~~not~~ many people have these days. That's   20c

a shame they did at least two things for which they should be remembered. They   20d

probably saved the labor movement in America, they definitely gave American folk   20a

music some of its most unforgettable songs. No one really knows how they got their

nickname almost everyone knows a song or two that they inspired.   20a

    The Wobblies were the members of the Industrial Workers of the World (IWW),

this union was a small but militant coalition of radical labor groups. The Wobblies   20d

could not get along with the major union groups of the day, in fact, they alienated most   20b

of those groups.

    The major unions disliked the Wobblies immensely, nevertheless they learned   20d

some valuable lessons from them. The first lesson was to avoid getting involved

in politics. If there was one thing the Wobblies hated more than capitalism, it was

politics. The Wobblies avoided politics for one good reason, they believed that political   20b

affiliation caused the death of unions. What else did the major unions learn, they   20c

learned to deal realistically with workers' problems. Major unions also learned new

recruiting techniques from the Wobblies. In addition, they copied the Wobblies in

devoting their energy to nuts-and-bolts issues affecting the workers.

    The major unions never recognized their debt to the Wobblies, the debt was still   20a

there for historians to see. Historians began to compile the story of the American labor

unions, then they finally recognized the contributions of the Wobblies.   20d

Van Goor and Hacker, *Developmental Exercises for Rules for Writers*, 7th ed. (Boston: Bedford, 2012)

20-1 | Run-on sentences: Guided practice   **53**

EXERCISE 20-2 ◆ Run-on sentences

To read about this topic, see section 20 in *Rules for Writers*, Seventh Edition.

One sentence in each of the following pairs is a run-on sentence. Find and correct the error, using an effective revision strategy. Mark the correct sentence "OK." Example:

        Although
a.   Joe Hill may not have been the first martyr of the labor movement, ~~however,~~ he was certainly its most skillful worker with words and music.

b.   Before his arrest in 1914 for killing a grocer in Salt Lake City, Joe Hill was simply the Swedish immigrant Joseph Hillstrom; no one knew or cared much about him.   *OK*

1. a.   Ralph Chaplin was the only person who wrote anything about Joe Hill before Hill's execution, he jotted down just a few notes based on an interview with a drunken sailor.

    b.   Extensive historical research has not confirmed or denied those notes because researchers have turned up quite different stories.

2. a.   All the evidence introduced at Hill's trial was circumstantial; furthermore, the dead man's son, who had witnessed the murder, refused to identify Hill as the gunman.

    b.   Did the state hide evidence it certainly seemed that way.

3. a.   One Wobbly told the police that he had been with Joe Hill in another location on the night of the murder, he also told a detective he could prove Hill's innocence.

    b.   That man was promptly arrested and held in jail for the duration of the trial.

4. a.   At the end of the trial, the man was released and ordered to leave the state.

    b.   Hill's own attorneys did not do much to help him their attitude was as negative as that of the prosecutors.

5. a.   Because of their negative attitude, Hill discharged both of the attorneys who were supposed to be defending him.

    b.   "I have three prosecutors here, I intend to get rid of two of them," he said.

Van Goor and Hacker, *Developmental Exercises for Rules for Writers*, 7th ed. (Boston: Bedford, 2012)

20-2 | Run-on sentences **55**

6. a. The state never showed a motive for the murder; furthermore, much evidence that Hill's attorneys could have used was never introduced.

    b. How did Hill get that bullet wound in his chest, he told the doctor he had gotten it in a fight over a woman.

7. a. The doctor who treated Hill was not asked to testify about medical aspects of the case, as a matter of fact, his testimony probably would have prevented Hill's conviction.

    b. Protests about Hill's conviction came from all over the world, but they were ignored.

8. a. Important political figures tried to help Hill, hoping until the last minute that they could save him.

    b. The Swedish consul pleaded for him, President Wilson sent telegrams to the governor of Utah.

9. a. Legend has it that Hill's last words before the firing squad were "Don't mourn for me; organize," in fact, he said, "Yes, aim! Let her go! Fire!"

    b. If Joe Hill is known at all today, it is probably because of Joe Glazer, his guitar, and the song "Joe Hill."

10. a. Glazer was not the composer of "Joe Hill" its composers were Earl Robinson and Alfred Hayes.

    b. Glazer, however, made the song known across America, singing it at banquets as well as on picket lines.

Van Goor and Hacker, *Developmental Exercises for Rules for Writers*, 7th ed. (Boston: Bedford, 2012)

EXERCISE 20-3 ◆ Run-on sentences

To read about this topic, see section 20 in *Rules for Writers*, Seventh Edition.

Correct each run-on sentence using the method of revision suggested in brackets. Example:

> with whom
> **From his death cell, Joe Hill sent a letter to Big Bill Haywood, he had worked ~~with~~**
>
> **~~Haywood~~ in the early days of the IWW. [Restructure the sentence; see 20d.]**

1. Joe Hill's final letter to Big Bill Haywood had only five sentences, it contained one line about his death, one admonition to Haywood, and three comments related to Hill's burial. [Use a colon; see 20b.]

2. He commented briefly about his death he said, "I die like a true rebel." [Restructure the sentence; see 20d.]

3. Hill told Haywood, "Don't waste time mourning for me, organize instead." [Use a semicolon; see 20b.]

4. Hill, in prison in Utah, did not want to be buried in that state, he asked Haywood to haul his body into Wyoming, a hundred miles away. [Use a coordinating conjunction; see 20a.]

5. Hill gave only one reason for requesting burial in Wyoming, he said, "I don't want to be found dead in Utah." [Make two sentences; see 20c.]

6. On the night before his execution, he wrote a final poem, in it he made two requests. [Restructure the sentence; see 20d.]

7. He wanted his body to be cremated, he wanted his ashes to be allowed to blow freely around the earth. [Use a coordinating conjunction; see 20a.]

8. Here's how he said it in his poem,

   Let the merry breezes blow
   My dust to where some flowers grow.
   Perhaps some fading flower then
   Would come to life and bloom again. [Use a colon; see 20b.]

9. Obviously, Joe Hill was not a great poet, however, he was clever with rhymes. [Use a semicolon; see 20b.]

10. Even in his will he managed to fit in a humorous rhyme,

    This is my last and final will.
    Good luck to all of you.
              — Joe Hill [Use a colon; see 20b.]

Van Goor and Hacker, *Developmental Exercises for Rules for Writers*, 7th ed. (Boston: Bedford, 2012)

20-3 | Run-on sentences **57**

EXERCISE 20-4 ◆ Run-on sentences

To read about this topic, see section 20 in *Rules for Writers*, Seventh Edition.

Correct each of the following run-on sentences in the way you think is most effective. Example:

> **Joe Hill was not buried in Utah ; he was not buried in Wyoming either.**

1. After Joe Hill's death, his body was sent to Chicago, a large auditorium was secured for the funeral services.

2. More than thirty thousand people overflowed the auditorium, they jammed the streets as they followed the funeral train to the cemetery.

3. Very few of these mourners knew Joe Hill personally, nevertheless, he was a true hero to them.

4. On that Thanksgiving Day of 1915, they knew that other people mourned him too they heard eulogies to him in nine different languages.

5. Those mourners and thousands like them sang his songs, because they did, Joe Hill's name lived on.

6. Hill's satirical, angry songs often had a surprising tenderness, it is no wonder that he was named poet laureate of the Wobbly movement.

7. In some ways, Joe Hill's death freed him, in other ways, he remains a prisoner.

8. Joe Hill did get part of his deathbed wish, his body was cremated.

9. He was cremated at the cemetery afterward his ashes were put in thirty envelopes and sent all over the world.

10. The IWW kept one envelope, the Department of Justice confiscated it in 1918 for use in a trial. Since the envelope was never returned, part of Joe Hill is still "in prison."

Van Goor and Hacker, *Developmental Exercises for Rules for Writers*, 7th ed. (Boston: Bedford, 2012)

EXERCISE 20-5 ◆ Run-on sentences: Guided review

Revise each run-on sentence in the following paragraphs using the method of revision suggested by the rule number in the margin. See section 20 of *Rules for Writers*, Seventh Edition. The first sentence has been revised for you.

> *Although he*
> ~~He~~ never calls them by name, John Steinbeck immortalizes the Wobblies in   20d
>
> *The Grapes of Wrath.* The novel is about the life of the Joad family. The Joads have   20d
>
> lost their farm during the Depression, the family has come to California seeking work.
>
> There is no permanent work for anyone, moreover, the money earned by picking crops   20b
>
> is not enough to feed the family.
>
> Union organizers have talked to the workers about organizing and striking.
>
> Tom, the oldest Joad son, has listened to them, however, he has not yet joined them.   20a
>
> Tom is in hiding because he has accidentally killed a man in a fight. He spends all
>
> his daylight hours alone, he has lots of time to think about his family's situation. Tom   20a
>
> becomes convinced that life is unfair for his people, he decides to leave the family, find   20d
>
> the union men, and work with them.
>
> He is inarticulate when he tries to explain to Ma what he hopes to do he   20c
>
> gropes for words to express his frustration and his hope. Ma asks him how she will
>
> know about him, she worries that he might get killed and she would not know. Tom's   20a
>
> reassurances are almost mystical: "Wherever they's a fight so hungry people can eat,
>
> I'll be there.... An' when our folks eat the stuff they raise an' live in the houses they
>
> build—why, I'll be there."
>
> If Tom had had a copy of the Wobblies' "little red song book," he could have
>
> found less mystical words. Every copy of the book contained the Wobblies' Preamble,
>
> the first sentence in the Preamble was unmistakably clear "The working class and the   20d, 20b
>
> employing class have nothing in common." Tom would have understood those words he   20b
>
> would have believed them, too.

EXERCISE 21-1 ◆ Subject-verb agreement: Guided practice

Circle the correct verb from each pair in parentheses. The numbers in the margin refer to relevant rules in section 21 of *Rules for Writers*, Seventh Edition. The first selection has been made for you; answers to this exercise appear in the back of this book.

Before reaching college, nearly everyone already (knows)/ know) several facts   21e

about fables. Most students know, for example, that fables are short stories that

(conveys / convey) a moral. They also know that fables nearly always have animal   21i

characters but that animal characters alone (is / are) not a signal that the story is a   21h

fable. They know of Aesop, to whom most familiar fables in Western culture (is / are)   21b

attributed. They know that there (is / are) generally only two or three characters in   21g

an Aesop fable and that a crowd of observers almost never (has / have) a role in his   21f

stories.

Most adults recognize that the subject matter of Aesop's fables is nearly always

the same. Once in a while, but not often, politics (is / are) highlighted in a story.   21j

Usually, however, Aesop's fables point out the value of common sense or make gentle

fun of human failings. Since neither foolish behavior nor human failings

(seems / seem) to be in short supply, Aesop's stories continue to be told. Besides, they   21d

attract a wide audience: Adults and children both (enjoy / enjoys) them. Everyone who   21c

has gone to school (is / are) supposed to know some of Aesop's fables. "The Fox and the   21e

Grapes," for instance, (is / are) familiar to many children as a story long before they   21k

understand its meaning.

Van Goor and Hacker, *Developmental Exercises for Rules for Writers*, 7th ed. (Boston: Bedford, 2012)

EXERCISE 21-2 ◆ Subject-verb agreement

To read about this topic, see section 21 in *Rules for Writers*, Seventh Edition.

Verbs in the following sentences are italicized. Underline the simple subject (or simple subjects) of each verb, and edit the verb to make it agree with the subject. Keep all verbs in the present tense. Do not change the three correct sentences. Example:

<u>**Many**</u> **of the morals or wise sayings from fables *has* become a part of our language.**

have

1. Phrases like "a wolf in sheep's clothing" *is used and understood* by many people.

2. The expression "a wolf in sheep's clothing" *comes* from one of Aesop's fables.

3. A flock of sheep and a hungry wolf *is* the main characters in the story.

4. After killing a sheep for their supper, the shepherd and his helpers *forgets* about the skin from the sheep.

5. The wolf, finding the discarded skin, *cover* himself with it.

6. Joining the flock, he *pretends* to be a mother looking for her lamb.

7. The flock *accept* him as a sheep.

8. Neither the sheep nor the shepherd *notice* the wolf at first.

9. Luring a lamb from the flock each day, the wolf *feeds* himself very well for a while.

10. Everyone hearing the story *understand* its warning: to beware of people pretending to be what they are not.

Van Goor and Hacker, *Developmental Exercises for Rules for Writers*, 7th ed. (Boston: Bedford, 2012)

21-2 | Subject-verb agreement **61**

EXERCISE 21-3 ◆ Subject-verb agreement

To read about this topic, see section 21 in *Rules for Writers*, Seventh Edition.

Each of the following sentences has two subjects and verbs (some of the subject-verb pairs are in subordinate structures). The simple subjects are italicized. Edit each incorrect verb to make it agree with its subject. Keep all verbs in the present tense. One subject-verb pair in each sentence is correct. Example:

> *is*
> "*Sour grapes*" ~~are~~ a common expression, but not *everyone* knows the origin of that phrase.

1. Aesop's *story* "The Fox and the Grapes" tells about a fox *who* try unsuccessfully to get some grapes.

2. There are a big *bunch* of grapes hanging over the top of a wall, and the *fox* is hot and thirsty.

3. A favorite *food* of his are grapes, and *he* leaps up to get some—without success.

4. Hoping that no *crowd* of friends are watching, the *fox* takes a running leap for the top of the wall.

5. Unsuccessful, the *fox* in the story tries again and again with the same result; neither his *cleverness* nor his high *leaps* is successful.

6. Embarrassed, the *fox* fears that *news* of his failures are going to give his friends something to tease him about.

7. The fox's *pride* and his *self-confidence* has suffered, so *he* claims not to want the grapes anyway.

8. The *fox*, stalking proudly off with his nose in the air, say that the *grapes* are sour.

9. *Everyone* know that the *fox* does not believe his own words.

10. To save their pride, *people* often pretends not to want what *they* cannot get.

Van Goor and Hacker, *Developmental Exercises for Rules for Writers*, 7th ed. (Boston: Bedford, 2012)

EXERCISE 21-4 ◆ Subject-verb agreement: Guided review

Circle the correct verb from each pair in parentheses. The numbers in the margin refer to relevant rules in section 21 of *Rules for Writers*, Seventh Edition. The first selection has been made for you.

From one of Aesop's lesser-known fables (comes / come) the question "Who's   21g

going to bell the cat?" The fable "Belling the Cat" describes the long battle between

mice and cats.

In the story, a committee of mice is appointed to find a way to keep the cat from

killing so many mice. Everyone on the committee (tries / try) to solve the problem.   21e

There (is / are) many committee meetings and much discussion, but in the end neither   21g

the committee nor its chairperson (is / are) able to make any good suggestions. Finally,   21d

the time comes for the committee to make its report at a public meeting. Embarrassed,

the committee (reports / report) its failure.   21f

At first, there is only silence; no one wants to accept the committee's report as

the final word on the problem. Then a little pip-squeak among the mice (suggests /   21b

suggest) tying a bell on the cat. The young mouse makes quite a speech in favor of his

idea. According to that mouse, statistics (shows / show) that no mice have ever been   21j

captured by a noisy cat. The mouse points out that his solution would not cost much;

a bell and a string (is / are) all the equipment needed to give the mice warning of the   21c

cat's approach. The mouse who makes the suggestion gets a round of applause. The

committee members, who (wishes / wish) that they had thought of the idea, are silent.   21i

Then a wise old mouse asks, "Who will bell the cat?" The experienced mice and the

young pip-squeak (is / are) silent.   21c

It is easy to make suggestions that other people (has / have) to carry out.   21a

Van Goor and Hacker, *Developmental Exercises for Rules for Writers*, 7th ed. (Boston: Bedford, 2012)

21-4 | Subject-verb agreement: Guided review   **63**

EXERCISE 22-1 ◆ Pronoun-antecedent agreement: Guided practice

Edit the following paragraphs for problems with pronoun-antecedent agreement. The numbers in the margin refer to relevant rules in section 22 of *Rules for Writers*, Seventh Edition. The first revision has been done for you; a suggested revision of this exercise appears in the back of this book.

Everyone has heard of Dorothy and Toto and their tornado "flight" from Kansas
Everyone also knows
to Oz. ~~They also know~~ that the Oz adventure was pure fantasy and that it ended   22a
happily. But another girl from Kansas took real flights all around the real world.

Whenever she landed safely after setting one of her many records, everyone rejoiced

and sent their congratulations to her. When she disappeared on her last flight, the   22a

whole world mourned. Not every pilot can claim they have that kind of following.   22a

Neighbors knew that Amelia Earhart would not be a typical "lady." A child as

curious, daring, and self-confident as Amelia was bound to stand out from her peers.

When she and her sister Muriel were young, girls were supposed to play with dolls. If

a girl played baseball or collected worms, they were called "tomboys" and were often   22a

punished. Boys and girls even had different kinds of sleds—the girls' sleds were

lightweight, impossible-to-steer box sleds.

But the Earhart family lived by their own rules. Amelia's father, whom she   22b

depended on for approval, bought Amelia the boys' sled she longed for. Many fast trips

down steep hills gave Amelia a foretaste of flying with the wind in her face.

The closest Amelia came to flying was on a homemade roller coaster. She and

her friends built it, using an old woodshed for the base of the ride. They started eight

feet off the ground and tried to sled down the slope without falling off. No one was

successful on their first attempt, but Amelia kept trying until she had a successful   22a

ride. Satisfied at last, she declared that the ride had felt "just like flying."

Van Goor and Hacker, *Developmental Exercises for Rules for Writers*, 7th ed. (Boston: Bedford, 2012)

EXERCISE 22-2 ◆ Pronoun-antecedent agreement

To read about this topic, see section 22 in *Rules for Writers*, Seventh Edition.

Five of the following word groups contain a problem with pronoun-antecedent agreement. Mark the correct sentences "OK" and edit the incorrect ones to eliminate the problem. Example:

> **During World War I, Amelia Earhart listened to wounded pilots' tales of adventure.** ~~**A pilot**~~ *Pilots*
> **would describe a particularly daring wartime adventure and joke about their ability to**
> **beat the odds.**

1. After World War I, Amelia Earhart took flying lessons. She learned quickly, but the lessons cost her most of her salary.

2. She wanted those lessons, so she worked two jobs to pay for them: She clerked for the telephone company and drove a dump truck for a sand and gravel company.

3. Members of her family pooled their funds to buy a gift—a little yellow biplane—for her twenty-fourth birthday celebration; it was the perfect gift.

4. Amelia Earhart soon learned that when someone owns a plane, they need a lot of money.

5. She sometimes executed dangerous maneuvers before her teacher was sure Amelia could handle it.

6. At first everyone could not believe their eyes when she deliberately put her plane into a spin.

7. Each spectator would gasp when they heard her cut the engine off in a spin.

8. But Amelia Earhart repeatedly pulled the plane out of its spin and landed safely, delighting everyone.

9. When an aviator wants to break records, they will work very hard.

10. Aviation record keepers had to make a new entry in the record books: They had seen Amelia Earhart fly 14,000 feet high.

Van Goor and Hacker, *Developmental Exercises for Rules for Writers*, 7th ed. (Boston: Bedford, 2012)

22-2 | Pronoun-antecedent agreement   **65**

EXERCISE 22-3 ◆ Pronoun-antecedent agreement

To read about this topic, see section 22 in *Rules for Writers*, Seventh Edition.

In each set of sentences, circle the letter of the sentence that has a problem with pronoun-antecedent agreement. Which of the other two sentences (both correct) do you prefer? Put a check mark next to that sentence. Example:

(a.) A college dropout often gets little respect for their choosing to leave school.

b. College dropouts often get little respect for their choosing to leave school.

✓ c. A college dropout often gets little respect for choosing to leave school.

1. a. Not everyone who drops out of college ruins their life.

   b. Not all students who drop out of college ruin their lives.

   c. Not all college dropouts ruin their lives.

2. a. Students sometimes discover that they don't like their chosen field.

   b. A student sometimes discovers that he or she doesn't like their chosen field.

   c. Students may lose interest in their chosen field.

3. a. People like Amelia, who quit school to learn to fly, must be very sure of themselves.

   b. Someone like Amelia, who quit school to learn to fly, must be very sure of themselves.

   c. Someone like Amelia, who quit school to learn to fly, must be very sure of herself or himself.

4. a. In their catalog, Columbia University offered a wide range of courses, but Flying Airplanes was not among them.

   b. Flying Airplanes was not among the wide range of courses offered in Columbia University's catalog.

   c. In its catalog, Columbia University offered a wide range of courses, but Flying Airplanes was not among them.

5. a. Amelia Earhart became a dropout any university would be proud to claim.

   b. Amelia Earhart became one of those dropouts any university would be proud to claim as theirs.

   c. Amelia Earhart became a dropout all universities would be proud to claim.

Van Goor and Hacker, *Developmental Exercises for Rules for Writers*, 7th ed. (Boston: Bedford, 2012)

EXERCISE 22-4 ◆ Pronoun-antecedent agreement: Guided review

Edit the following paragraphs for problems with pronoun-antecedent agreement. The numbers in the margin refer to relevant rules in section 22 of *Rules for Writers*, Seventh Edition. The first revision has been done for you.

When Amelia Earhart became the first woman to cross the Atlantic in a plane,

she got no money; she did get a free ride, fame, and job offers. Not ~~every flier~~ *all fliers* would   22a

think these rewards were enough for their time and trouble on the trip, but Amelia

Earhart was delighted with the whole experience. Afterward, a book she wrote about

that flight brought her another first: a publisher, a shrewd business manager, and

a husband—all in one man, George Putnam. (Putnam also understood her fierce

independence—not every man would sign a prenuptial agreement saying that their   22a

wife could have a divorce anytime she asked!)

The first national organization for "flying women," formed by Amelia Earhart

and a friend, recruited their members in the belief that every woman should follow   22b

her own interest. After all, who had made the first solo flight from Honolulu to the

United States? From Los Angeles to Mexico City? And from Mexico City to New

Jersey? It was she, Amelia Earhart. No woman ever did more to prove that they could   22a

handle jobs traditionally reserved for men.

Amelia Earhart's last "first" was never completed. When she tried to become the

first pilot to fly around the world at the equator, she disappeared somewhere over the

Pacific. The US government search covered more than 265,000 miles of air and sea

space, but they found nothing.   22a

In 1994, fifty-seven years after Amelia Earhart's disappearance, twelve-year-old

Vicki Van Meter became the youngest female pilot to fly across the Atlantic. She took

off from Augusta, Maine, from the very spot where Amelia Earhart had started her

flight across the Atlantic. When Van Meter landed safely in Glasgow, everyone offered

their congratulations, and Van Meter felt a special kinship with her predecessor,   22a

Amelia Earhart.

EXERCISE 23-1 ◆ Pronoun reference: Guided practice

Edit the following paragraphs to correct errors in pronoun reference. The numbers in the margin refer to relevant rules in section 23 of *Rules for Writers*, Seventh Edition. The first revision has been done for you; a suggested revision of this exercise appears in the back of this book.

George and Mary Jones lived in Memphis during the Civil War. They were
Being caught in the middle
sympathetic to the Union, but the city definitely favored the Confederates. ~~This~~ made   23b
the war years especially hard on them. They looked forward to a much better life after
the war.

At first, it seemed that they were going to have that better life. George got a job
as a labor organizer, and Mary stayed at home to care for their four healthy children.
Then came yellow fever. In nine months, Mary went from a happy wife and mother to
a despondent widow with no children. She had to find work. Because you must have   23d
some meaning for living, she needed work that she could care strongly about.

By 1900, Mary had become involved in union activities all over the United
States. She found her calling among the coal miners and their wives, which she   23a
followed for the next thirty years. Making friends with the workers and outwitting
private detectives, she held secret meetings to help them organize and plan strategy.   23a
In the newspaper, it often reported her ability to outwit and outlast mine bosses and   23d
lawyers as well as to reawaken courage in disconsolate workers.

Mary Jones spent many nights in jail, but often her jailers did not know what
to do with this attractive gray-haired woman whom the workers called "Mother." The
jailers' confusion simply amused Mary, who was far more used to jail than they could   23c
imagine.

Van Goor and Hacker, *Developmental Exercises for Rules for Writers*, 7th ed. (Boston: Bedford, 2012)

EXERCISE 23-2 ◆ Pronoun reference

To read about this topic, see section 23 in *Rules for Writers*, Seventh Edition.

Six of the following sentences contain faulty pronoun references. Find the faulty references and fix them. Mark the correct sentences "OK." Example:

> *and this job*
> **Mother Jones got a job working in the textile mills, ~~which~~ made her conscious of how**
> **women workers were mistreated.**

1. When Mother Jones started working in the textile mills at the turn of the twentieth century, she saw "the little gray ghosts," the child laborers which worked from sunup to sundown.

2. Children as young as six scooted along the floor oiling and cleaning the huge whirring looms, which often devoured a child's fingers or hand.

3. Mother Jones once led a delegation of three hundred children from Philadelphia to New York to dramatize their plight; in some of the newspapers, they called her "the greatest female agitator in the country."

4. The speeches Mother Jones made about child labor were among her best: They called for legislation to forbid labor practices dangerous to children's health.

5. When Mother Jones asked for permission to bring three of the children to meet with President Theodore Roosevelt in New York, she was refused. It saddened her because she had hoped for the president's help.

6. Mother Jones asked again and was again refused. This second one saddened her even more, but she still did not consider the trip a failure.

7. She told the children and their parents that they had been successful.

8. Public awareness, which she felt would help the children, gradually began to increase.

9. Thousands of people had learned about the children's plight, which was bound to affect their thinking about child labor laws.

10. Mother Jones's optimism had another basis as well: The children would remember—and they would grow up.

Van Goor and Hacker, *Developmental Exercises for Rules for Writers*, 7th ed. (Boston: Bedford, 2012)

23-2 | Pronoun reference **69**

EXERCISE 23-3 ◆ Pronoun reference

To read about this topic, see section 23 in *Rules for Writers*, Seventh Edition.

Problem pronouns are italicized in the following paragraphs. Edit the paragraphs to eliminate any misunderstandings these pronouns might cause. You may need to restructure some sentences. Example:

> *workers*
> **In the mines, ~~you~~ didn't get much chance at the good life.**
>   ^

Mother Jones was determined to change the intolerable working conditions in the mines. After digging coal in twelve-to-fourteen-hour shifts, *they* found in their miners' pay envelopes not US currency but scrip, paper money that was honored only by the mining company. Local merchants had no use for the scrip, so *they* couldn't use it to buy food, clothes, or anything else. Workers, therefore, had to rent their homes from the company and buy their supplies at company stores. In company-run schools, the workers' children were taught by teachers *that* were hired by the company. *Their* families listened to company-paid ministers in company-owned churches.

Songwriter Merle Travis may have broken a pronoun reference rule, but he certainly summed *it* up neatly in one of his songs:

> You load sixteen tons, what do you get?
>
> Another day older and deeper in debt.
>
> St. Peter, don't you call me 'cause I can't go.
>
> I owe my soul to the company store.

[What pronoun does Travis use in a way that would be inappropriate in formal written English?]

Van Goor and Hacker, *Developmental Exercises for Rules for Writers*, 7th ed. (Boston: Bedford, 2012)

EXERCISE 23-4 ◆ Pronoun reference: Guided review

Edit the following paragraphs to correct errors in pronoun reference. The numbers in the margin refer to relevant rules in section 23 of *Rules for Writers*, Seventh Edition. The first revision has been done for you.

Coal miners' struggles turned into actual war in the Kanawha Valley of West

miners

Virginia, where ~~they~~ were striking. The mine owners dominated the courts and the   23c

newspapers; they did not need to worry about the law or public opinion. Although

the miners did not want to accept this, they were often forced to face it. Guards   23b

used violent tactics to maintain the mine owners' control, once spraying strikers'

tent colonies with machine-gun fire and kicking a pregnant woman so hard that her

unborn child died in the womb.

Mother Jones urged the miners to fight while she tried to gain the ear of the

governor, federal lawmakers, and the public. In records of the fight, it says that two   23d

thousand miners came from outside the valley to help in the battle. The state militia

was called in, but the owners got control of the militia soon after it arrived. En route

to the state legislature to ask them for help, Mother Jones was kidnapped by soldiers,   23c

held incommunicado, put in solitary confinement, and tried by a military court. When

the new governor of West Virginia, Henry D. Hatfield, investigated, he found a soldier

guarding an eighty-year-old pneumonia-ridden woman that had a 104-degree fever.   23e

Word about the Kanawha situation got out, but Governor Hatfield acted first.

Out of his work came the Hatfield Agreement. This document, which historians of the

labor movement consider a major advance for workers in the United States, forced the

companies to recognize the union and to shorten the workday. Even more important,

it stipulated that companies must pay wages in US currency. He also guaranteed   23a

civilians the right to civil, not military, trials and dismissed all sentences the military

court had imposed—including the twenty-year prison term it had set for Mother

Jones.

EXERCISE 24-1 ◆ Pronoun and noun case: Guided practice

Circle the correct pronoun or noun from each pair of words in parentheses. The numbers in the margin refer to relevant rules in section 24 of *Rules for Writers*, Seventh Edition. The first selection has been made for you; answers to this exercise appear in the back of this book.

When union organizer Mother Jones went to Colorado in 1913, no one worked

harder than (she / her) to help the miners. (They / Them) and their families lived in   24d, 24a

company houses that the company's own reports called unfit for human habitation.

Although Mother Jones wanted to help the miners, she saw no way to get the two

groups, the owners and (they / them), together.   24c

Mother Jones did not give up. When threatening posters went up all over town,

she laughed and encouraged the miners with slogans like "(We / Us) miners have got   24e

to stick together." When Mother Jones appealed to the governor for help, no one really

expected the governor and (she / her) to agree, but many people hoped he would help   24f

somehow. Instead, he simply ordered her out of the state.

The miners were evicted from their houses. (They / Them) and their families   24a

moved into tents. After company guards raked the tents with machine-gun fire, the

miners dug pits under the tents. The pits were deep enough to protect their families

and (they / them) from gunfire, but at Ludlow, guards set fire to the tents. Whole   24b

families were roasted to death in the pits. When word of the massacre got out, workers

from all over the state swarmed to Ludlow. No one was ever as angry as (they / them).

They set fire to company buildings, fought the state and company troops, and took   24d

over the nearby mines and towns.

Mother Jones went to Washington to ask President Wilson for help. Although

she and (he / him) did not agree on all points, he did establish a review board and   24a

send in federal troops to restore order. The companies did not like the (president /   24g

president's) sending in troops and absolutely refused to accept the findings of the

review board. Eventually, the miners went back to work under almost the same

conditions as before. Disappointed as they were, they knew that it was (she / her),   24a

Mother Jones, who was the most disappointed of all.

Van Goor and Hacker, *Developmental Exercises for Rules for Writers*, 7th ed. (Boston: Bedford, 2012)

EXERCISE 24-2 ◆ Pronoun and noun case

To read about this topic, see section 24 in *Rules for Writers*, Seventh Edition.

Six of the following sentences have errors in pronoun or noun case. Find and fix the errors. Mark "OK" next to the sentences that have no errors. Example:

> Mother Jones liked to discuss union affairs with her friend Terence Powderly; she and ~~him~~ *he* could argue for hours about the best approach to a problem.

1. People all over the world knew about Mother Jones. Wherever she went, she was invited into their homes and their workplaces.

2. Once when she was traveling with Fred Mooney in Mexico, a crowd stopped the train and urged Mooney and she to open the train window.

3. Mooney and she were not sure whether they should open the window, but they decided to do so. When they did, she and him both were showered with red carnations and blue violets.

4. Although the people gave the flowers to both him and her, the flowers were meant as gifts in honor of "Madre Yones," as the people called her.

5. The trip to Mexico was exhausting, but it was she, over ninety years old, who never ran out of energy.

6. When Mooney fretted about her health, it was her who laughed and proposed that they get on with their sightseeing.

7. No one was more excited than her about the idea of a Pan-American Federation of Labor, an organization that would unite workers from Canada to South America.

8. The president of Mexico was as pleased as her at the idea of bringing together all the working people in the hemisphere.

9. "This is the beginning of a new day for us working people," exclaimed Mother Jones.

10. It was a day Mother Jones long remembered; years later it brought happy smiles to she and her friends whenever they saw carnations and violets or thought of that day's events.

Van Goor and Hacker, *Developmental Exercises for Rules for Writers*, 7th ed. (Boston: Bedford, 2012)

24-2 | Pronoun and noun case **73**

EXERCISE 24-3 ◆ Pronoun and noun case

To read about this topic, see section 24 in *Rules for Writers*, Seventh Edition.

Some of the personal pronouns in this passage are italicized; six of them are not in the correct case. The first one has been corrected for you. Find and correct the other five.

Though ~~*her*~~ *she* and a friend would occasionally work together on the friend's campaign, Mother Jones avoided politics most of the time. *She*, the agitator, had no more interest in politics and political science than *her*, the labor organizer, had in economic theory. Mother Jones understood one kind of economics, the kind that dealt with wages, benefits, and the cost of bread and housing. The here-and-now problems of the poor called to Mother Jones so strongly that *she* had to do what *she* could to stop the injustice she saw around *her*.

Surprisingly, Mother Jones was not a supporter of woman suffrage. When the fight to win women's right to vote came along, it was not *her* who supported it. *Herself* and her people were the working classes, both men and women, and neither *she* nor *them* had much patience for the "society women" who led the movement. As far as Mother Jones was concerned, well-dressed women parading down the city streets carrying placards and banners did not help working men and women obtain a decent life. Mother Jones objected to *them* spending time and energy and money on activities that would not help her kind of people. Nor was *she* interested in helping a cause that would benefit only women; her concern was for all workers, regardless of gender. *She* seemed not to understand that the votes of the miners' wives might do as much to help the working men as *her* agitating and organizing did.

Van Goor and Hacker, *Developmental Exercises for Rules for Writers*, 7th ed. (Boston: Bedford, 2012)

EXERCISE 24-4 ◆ Pronoun and noun case: Guided review

Circle the correct pronoun or noun from each pair of words in parentheses. The numbers in the margin refer to relevant rules in section 24 of *Rules for Writers*, Seventh Edition. The first selection has been made for you.

Eventually, labor organizer Mother Jones began to think about her death. She wrote her autobiography and made plans for her burial, but she could not have dreamed how her name would be kept alive many years after her death.

(She / Her) and an editor friend began her autobiography when Mother Jones   24a
was ninety-two. Even with her friend working as hard as (she / her), Mother Jones   24d
found writing to be a grinding, demanding chore. Annoyed with her (friend / friend's)   24g
trying to make her remember details of her youth, she covered the first thirty years of her life in a few paragraphs. She had trouble remembering even the later years, confusing names and occasionally mixing up dates. She was never confused, however, about her conviction that working people were being unfairly treated. Nor did she doubt the necessity for (she / her) and her friends to help redress the wrongs done to   24f
working people.

Mother Jones planned to be buried in a place special to her. Back in 1898, four miners had been killed during a strike in Mount Olive, Illinois, and no cemetery in town would allow the bodies of these men to be buried on its land. So the union bought its own cemetery to bury them and others like them. For Mother Jones, burial in Miners Cemetery, Mount Olive, Illinois, was a way to say "(We / Us) working people   24e
have got to stick together" even after her death.

She would have been puzzled by a memorial honoring her work. In the mid-twentieth century, a group of writers decided to publish a magazine devoted to exposing fraud and injustice in society. (They / Them) and their friends named this   24a
new publication *Mother Jones*. Mother Jones might not have appreciated the accolades it won or its citation by the *American Journalism Review* as "best in the business for investigative reporting," but she would have recognized at once the woman first listed under the journal's masthead: "Mother Jones (1830–1930)—Orator, Union Organizer, and Hellraiser."

EXERCISE 25-1 ◆ *Who* and *whom*: Guided practice

Circle the correct pronoun from each pair in parentheses. The numbers in the margin refer to relevant rules in section 25 of *Rules for Writers*, Seventh Edition. The first selection has been made for you; answers to this exercise appear in the back of this book.

Have you ever heard of George Leroy Parker? You probably have; you just don't think so because you don't know (who)/ whom) George Leroy Parker really was. He   **25a**

was born on a Utah ranch in 1867. There were several cowhands on the ranch, and some of them had other jobs as well. One or two did a bit of farming, others went in for gambling, and one was a horse thief and cattle rustler. Of them all, (who / whom)   **25b**

did young George find most attractive? George never had any question about (who /   **25a**

whom) he admired most on the ranch. (Who / Whom) else would it be but Mike, the   **25b**

horse thief and cattle rustler? George was so impressed by Mike that years later he would tell stories about Mike's exploits to (whoever / whomever) would listen. Mike   **25a**

was the man George was eternally grateful to because he taught George how to ride and shoot. George was so grateful, in fact, that he took that man's last name for his own. He wanted to honor Mike Cassidy, the man (who / whom) he admired above all   **25a**

others.

[*Note*: Sometimes the pronoun *whom* may be dropped without loss of clarity. Are there any *whom*s in this paragraph that you might choose to drop?]

Van Goor and Hacker, *Developmental Exercises for Rules for Writers*, 7th ed. (Boston: Bedford, 2012)

EXERCISE 25-2 ◆ *Who* and *whom*

To read about this topic, see section 25 in *Rules for Writers*, Seventh Edition.

One sentence in each of the following pairs uses *who* and *whom* correctly and the other does not. Put "OK" after the correct sentence and correct the other one. Example:

   a.   People who deliberately change their last names do so for specific reasons.   *OK*

                                                     whom
   b.   Sometimes they are hiding from people ~~who~~ they have harmed.

1.   a.   It is unusual for a man to change his last name to honor someone who he admires.

     b.   George Leroy Parker became George Cassidy when he named himself for the man who had taught him the most.

2.   a.   One day George said good-bye to Mike Cassidy, who was leaving for Mexico.

     b.   The lawmen who Mike planned to outwit did not catch up with him this time.

3.   a.   George decided to join up with whoever he could find to try a train robbery.

     b.   He found the McCarty brothers and Matt Warner, to whom a robbery sounded like a good idea.

4.   a.   The gang underestimated who they would be dealing with.

     b.   The guard whom they threatened refused to open the safe.

5.   a.   The gang then voted on whether to rob the passengers, whom they had not originally intended to disturb.

     b.   The "no" votes won, so the gang left the passengers to wonder whom these vote-taking train robbers were.

[*Note*: Sometimes the pronoun *whom* may be dropped without loss of clarity. Are there any *whom*s in the preceding sentences that you might choose to drop?]

Van Goor and Hacker, *Developmental Exercises for Rules for Writers*, 7th ed. (Boston: Bedford, 2012)

25-2 | *Who* and *whom*   **77**

EXERCISE 25-3 ♦ *Who* and *whom*

To read about this topic, see section 25 in *Rules for Writers*, Seventh Edition.

Edit the following sentences to eliminate errors in the use of *who* and *whom*. Mark correct sentences "OK." Example:

> **George Cassidy, who was later known as Butch, robbed his first bank in 1889.**   *OK*

1. George Cassidy, who had already decided to rob the First National Bank of Denver, had a
    problem: Who could he find as a partner?

2. Maybe one of his old buddies who now lived in Star Valley, an almost perfect hideout, would
    be a partner on whom he could depend.

3. Whom else could it be but Tom McCarty, with whom George had tried his first train robbery?

4. When the robbers threatened the bank president with a bottle they said contained
    nitroglycerin, others said it was only water. The bank president didn't know who to believe
    because he couldn't tell whom was lying.

5. Actually, it was water, but who could have been sure of that?

Van Goor and Hacker, *Developmental Exercises for Rules for Writers*, 7th ed. (Boston: Bedford, 2012)

EXERCISE 25-4 ◆ *Who* and *whom*: Guided review

Circle the correct pronoun from each pair in parentheses. The numbers in the margin refer to section 25 of *Rules for Writers*, Seventh Edition. The first selection has been made for you.

George Cassidy got his nickname Butch from the people he served during one of

the few times he earned an honest living. The people George Cassidy worked for from

1890 to 1892 knew him as an honest worker. The available records don't show (who / whom)   25a

trained him for his job—butchering sheep, hogs, and steers. (Whoever / Whomever)   25a

had trained him had done it well. It was obvious to (whoever / whomever) looked at his   25a

work that George Cassidy knew how to handle a knife. His customers, (who / whom)   25a

he may well have robbed later, were satisfied with his work. They probably did not

realize how famous—or infamous—their butcher was to become. Even if Butch didn't

know which townspeople had given him his name, obviously he liked it; he used it for

the rest of his life. (Who / Whom) today hasn't heard of Butch Cassidy? (Who / Whom)   25b, 25b

did director George Roy Hill choose as the hero of one of his most popular films?

Van Goor and Hacker, *Developmental Exercises for Rules for Writers*, 7th ed. (Boston: Bedford, 2012)

25-4 | *Who* and *whom*: Guided review   **79**

EXERCISE 26-1 ◆ Adjectives and adverbs: Guided practice

Edit the following paragraphs for correct use of adjectives and adverbs. The numbers in the margin refer to relevant rules in section 26 of *Rules for Writers*, Seventh Edition. The first revision has been done for you; answers to this exercise appear in the back of this book.

Novelists have often used their storytelling talents to influence people's

thinking. Charles Dickens did it in nineteenth-century England. From *David*

Copperfield to *Oliver Twist*, book after book depicted the plight of the poor and other

really

~~real~~ unfortunate members of society. Harriet Beecher Stowe did it in nineteenth-   26b
  ^

century America, but with not hardly as many books. Her *Uncle Tom's Cabin* depicted   26e

slavery so well that the book strongly influenced antislavery sentiments in the decade

before the Civil War.

Harriet Beecher Stowe considered slavery sinful and wanted her book to help

end slavery quick and peaceful. People first read parts of the novel ten years before the   26b

beginning of the war. An abolitionist magazine published the book a few chapters at a

time, hoping the effect of the story would make readers feel so badly about slavery that   26c

they would rally to the abolitionist cause. Many people, reading *Uncle Tom's Cabin*

installment by installment, did become convinced that nothing could be worser than   26d

living in slavery on a southern plantation.

None of the abolitionists, who devoted their energy to abolishing slavery,

expected a more perfect world when the book itself was published in 1852. But they   26d

certainly hoped that the book would be influential. It was. Of all the novels published

that year, it was the top seller on both sides of the Atlantic. Its popularity was good

news for the abolitionists. Harriet Beecher Stowe's wish had come true.

Van Goor and Hacker, *Developmental Exercises for Rules for Writers*, 7th ed. (Boston: Bedford, 2012)

EXERCISE 26-2 ◆ Adjectives and adverbs

To read about this topic, see section 26 in *Rules for Writers*, Seventh Edition.

The two sentences in each of the following pairs are grammatically correct. The sentences have different meanings because one uses an adjective, the other an adverb. Read both sentences carefully to understand their meaning. Then circle the letter of the sentence that answers the question; be prepared to explain what the other sentence means. Example:

Which sentence means that southerners thought the book itself was dishonest?

a. **Many southerners did not consider *Uncle Tom's Cabin* honest.**

b. **Many southerners did not consider *Uncle Tom's Cabin* honestly.**

1. In which sentence did the people do a poor job of judging?

   a. Those people judged Mrs. Stowe's depiction of slave life inaccurate.

   b. Those people judged Mrs. Stowe's depiction of slave life inaccurately.

2. Which sentence says that the slaves had trouble finding the escape routes?

   a. Most slaves did not find their escape routes easy.

   b. Most slaves did not find their escape routes easily.

3. In which sentence do northerners think Stowe herself was honest?

   a. Most northerners believed Mrs. Stowe honest.

   b. Most northerners honestly believed Mrs. Stowe.

4. In which sentence did the judges think that some people had more rights than others?

   a. Southern judges did not consider all people equal.

   b. Southern judges did not consider all people equally.

5. Which sentence says that the overseers were looking scared?

   a. Rumors of escaping slaves made overseers look anxious when their slaves were out of sight.

   b. Rumors of escaping slaves made overseers look anxiously when their slaves were out of sight.

Van Goor and Hacker, *Developmental Exercises for Rules for Writers*, 7th ed. (Boston: Bedford, 2012)

26-2 | Adjectives and adverbs **81**

EXERCISE 26-3 ◆ Adjectives and adverbs

To read about this topic, see section 26 in *Rules for Writers*, Seventh Edition.

Six of the adjectives and adverbs in the following paragraphs are not used correctly. The first one has been corrected. Find and correct the other five.

      Uncle Tom's Cabin was ~~real~~ ^{really} popular, even though it was a very long book. When it was

published as a serial in the abolitionist magazine *National Era* in 1851 and 1852, people probably

read all of it. But when the novel was published as a book, many people did not have enough

time to read it. Since it had been a best-seller, enterprising publishers brought out new, abridged

versions for more faster reading. By the end of the Civil War, many people knew the story of *Uncle*

Tom's Cabin only from these shorter versions of it—both novels and plays.

      Unfortunately, their knowledge was not only incomplete; it was distorted. Publishers left out

important sections of this most priceless story. For example, in the book, Uncle Tom works for three

different owners, two of whom treat him fairly good. But in the shortened versions of the story,

Tom works for only one owner, who treats him very cruel. Even insensitive readers rightly found

that cruel owner, Simon Legree, vicious and judged all slave owners by him. In addition, what had

been a subplot in the novel—the story of George, Eliza, their baby, and the family's attempted

escape to freedom in Canada—became a major portion of the story. Playwrights favored such

dramatic subplots and incidents because they were easily dramatized.

      Modern readers are often real surprised when they read the entire novel, a book that

American critic Edmund Wilson called "a much more remarkable book than one had ever been

allowed to suspect."

Van Goor and Hacker, *Developmental Exercises for Rules for Writers*, 7th ed. (Boston: Bedford, 2012)

EXERCISE 26-4 ◆ Adjectives and adverbs: Guided review

Edit the following paragraph for correct use of adjectives and adverbs. The numbers in the margin refer to relevant rules in section 26 of *Rules for Writers*, Seventh Edition. The first revision has been done for you.

Playwrights often find popular novels suitable for the stage. Produced as a

play, *Uncle Tom's Cabin* was the ~~successfulest~~ *most successful* stage play of the 1800s. The play used   26d

only the real dramatic portions of the novel and therefore somewhat slanted its basic   26b

message. Even worse than the plays were the "Tom Shows" that toured small towns

all over the North; these shows didn't contain scarcely anything but the violent scenes.   26e

Audiences felt very badly when they watched George and Eliza's desperate escape   26c

over the ice with their baby. Dramatists played on their viewers' sympathy with the

plight of this slave family. Viewers hoped until the very end that the family's escape

would work out perfect. Distortion was bad in both the plays and the Tom Shows, but   26b

it was worse in the Tom Shows, which turned this most unique story of slavery in the   26d

South into little more than propaganda. Particularly moving scenes from the story

continue to be used in plays and musicals. *The King and I* incorporated several. If a

modern movie is ever made from *Uncle Tom's Cabin*, the movie could very well reflect

the same distortions present in the old plays and the Tom Shows—and might be just

as popular.

Van Goor and Hacker, *Developmental Exercises for Rules for Writers*, 7th ed. (Boston: Bedford, 2012)

26-4 | Adjectives and adverbs: Guided review   **83**

EXERCISE 27-1 ◆ Verb forms: Guided practice

Correct any nonstandard verb forms in the following paragraphs. The numbers in the margin refer to relevant rules in sections 27a to 27e of *Rules for Writers*, Seventh Edition. The first revision has been done for you; an answer to this exercise appears in the back of this book.

                                    don't

Most Americans today ~~doesn't~~ realize that the American democratic system did   27c

not always include African Americans and women. The constitutional amendments

pass after the Civil War granted former slaves and all native-born African American   27d

men full voting rights, but the new amendments ignored women. Women had to wait

much longer—more than half a century—to be gave the right to vote.   27a

    Some individual states allowed women to vote as early as 1900, but by

1910 women activists decided to focus their energy on a federal amendment.

When Woodrow Wilson became president in 1913, women demonstrated along the

inauguration route, marching and holding signs demanding the vote for women. Then

in 1917, Alice Paul and a militant faction of the suffrage movement picketed the

White House and even chained themselves to fences. When they were threaten and   27d

attacked by male mobs, police ignored the men and arrested the women. In prison,

the women endured filthy cells, force-feeding when they gone on a hunger strike, and   27a

ill treatment. Some women was restrained for many hours in uncomfortable positions   27a

with their arms high over their heads. One angry official repeatedly ask a doctor to   27d

declare one or more of the women insane. (The doctor refused.)

    President Wilson a man with major problems—a war abroad and women   27e

fighting for their rights at home. At first he tolerated the women picketers; he even

send coffee out to them. Then he just wanted the women to lie down their signs and   27a, 27b

banners and go home. But the increasing pressure from moderate and radical voices

in the movement as well as public outrage over the women's prison treatment finally

force Wilson to support a constitutional amendment for women's voting rights.   27d

Van Goor and Hacker, *Developmental Exercises for Rules for Writers*, 7th ed. (Boston: Bedford, 2012)

EXERCISE 27-2 ◆ Verb forms

To read about this topic, see sections 27a to 27e in *Rules for Writers*, Seventh Edition.

Edit the following paragraphs for missing *-ed* endings and incorrect forms of irregular verbs. The first revision has been done for you. You should make ten more.

      led
Women who ~~leaded~~ the suffrage movement never used violence, but they thought of themselves as waging a war. They tried different strategies in different places and coordinated their various attacks. Some concentrated on state and local voting rights for women; others work for national suffrage. In Washington, DC, they picketed, demonstrated, and builded and maintained "perpetual watchfires" in which they burned the speeches on democracy that President Wilson was giving in Europe.

      When the protesters were arrested at the White House in 1917, police had to use their personal cars to carry the many prisoners they arrest. After the women and some of their supporters were tried and found guilty, the judge got so tired of sentencing them that when he reached twenty-six, he dismiss all the others.

      The women's organizing and demonstrating finally paid off. On May 21, 1919, the House of Representatives passed the Nineteenth Amendment, giving women the right to vote, and sended it to the Senate. On June 4, the Senate approved it and passed it along to the states for ratification.

      Women's groups keeped up the pressure on the states during the long, tense ratification process. When, after more than a year, thirty-five states had ratified the amendment, it all come down to one man's vote in Tennessee. Who do history remember as the hero of ratification? A young legislator named Harry Burn, who cast the tie-breaking vote. On August 24, the governor of Tennessee certified the vote and sent the results to Washington.

      The US secretary of state had tell his staff to wake him as soon as the certificate arrived. He wanted to avoid a formal signing in the presence of the campaigning women. Nevertheless, on August 26, 1920, more than seventy years after women had first began to organize for suffrage, it was now official: Women in the United States had the right to vote.

Van Goor and Hacker, *Developmental Exercises for Rules for Writers*, 7th ed. (Boston: Bedford, 2012)

27-2 | Verb forms **85**

EXERCISE 27-3 ◆ Verb forms

To read about this topic, see sections 27a to 27e in *Rules for Writers*, Seventh Edition.

Edit the following paragraphs to correct problems with *-s* and *-ed* verb forms. The first revision has been done for you. You should make ten more.

               have
     Many historians ~~has~~ agreed that the woman suffrage movement in the United States

is rooted in the Seneca Falls Convention of 1848. The convention was organize by Elizabeth

Cady Stanton and Lucretia Mott, after Mott was denied a seat as a delegate at an antislavery

convention in London.

     The Seneca Falls Convention is best known for a document produce by Stanton called the

Declaration of Sentiments. Stanton's declaration remain one of the most important documents in

American women's history. Modeled on the Declaration of Independence (1776), the Declaration of

Sentiments list eighteen grievances—but these are grievances of women against their treatment

by men and male-dominated society. Stanton's declaration explicitly state that "all men and

women are created equal" and that women "demand the equal station to which they are entitled."

     A modern reader don't have to read more than a few sentences of each document to see the

similarities between the two. In fact, it have been said that the Declaration of Sentiments might

have been rejected if its format hadn't seemed so familiar to those who attended the convention.

The Declaration of Independence demand that men in America, like men in England, be

represented in government. The Declaration of Sentiments argue that women, like men, should be

represented in government. The women's document go so far as to suggest that American women

should have the right to vote. In 1848, this idea was shocking—so shocking that it would take

seventy-two years for women's right to vote to become a reality.

Van Goor and Hacker, *Developmental Exercises for Rules for Writers*, 7th ed. (Boston: Bedford, 2012)

EXERCISE 27-4 ◆ Verb forms: Guided review

Correct any nonstandard verb use in the following paragraphs. The numbers in the margin refer to relevant rules in sections 27a to 27e of *Rules for Writers*, Seventh Edition. The first revision has been done for you.

Today's American woman in a voting booth probably ~~don't~~ *doesn't* know how hard it was   27c

to win her the right to be there. It took thousands of women nearly a hundred years

to win that freedom for today's female voter. Many of those women who worked for

suffrage are no longer knowed, but their names should never be losted to history.   27a, 27a

From the first organized call for woman suffrage in 1848 through the end of the

nineteenth century, feminists such as Elizabeth Cady Stanton, Lucretia Mott, Lucy

Stone, and Susan B. Anthony remained strong voices for women's rights. The next

generation of activists included Harriet Blatch, the youngest daughter of Stanton,

who carry on her mother's work, and Alice Blackwell, the daughter of Lucy Stone, who   27d

continued to edit the *Women's Journal*, which her mother had founded.

In the early 1900s, the women took their cause to Washington. Just before

President Wilson's first inauguration in 1913, Inez Milholland, dressed in white and

riding a white horse, leaded eight thousand women in a march through Washington in   27a

support of the suffrage amendment. When she died at age thirty in 1916, a memorial

service was held for her in the US Capitol. She the first woman so honored.   27e

Alice Paul devoted her life to suffrage, planning and executing demonstrations

and campaigns. Friends worried that she never laid down to rest but was always   27b

working for the cause. Paul's arrest and mistreatment in prison in 1918 were

instrumental in gaining President Wilson's support for the Nineteenth Amendment.

Lucy Burns got involved in woman suffrage in England, leaving her studies at Oxford

to work for the suffrage movement. When she come to the United States in 1913,   27a

she led others in civil disobedience and was arrested and jailed several times. Carrie

Chapman Catt develop the strategy for the final years of the battle. Her strategy was   27d

called "The Winning Plan," and eventually it become just that.   27a

Today, most American women takes their right to vote for granted, unaware of   27c

the thousands of hands that opened the voting booth door for them.

EXERCISE 27-5 ◆ Verb tense and mood: Guided practice

Correct any tense or mood errors in the following paragraphs. The numbers in the margin refer to relevant rules in sections 27f and 27g of *Rules for Writers*, Seventh Edition. The first revision has been done for you; a suggested revision of this exercise appears in the back of this book.

    Almost everyone has heard about Aesop's fables, but most people know very little about Aesop himself. Most of what we know about Aesop is a mixture of hearsay and conjecture. We do know that he was a slave in Greece. One theory is that before he came to Greece he ^*had*^ lived in Ethiopia for most of his life and that "Aesop" is a much-shortened form of "the Ethiopian."   27f

    Aesop was not a storyteller then, though he would have loved to have spoken well enough to tell a good story. He stuttered so badly that he did not even try to talk. In one story we learn, however, that he *could* communicate. A neighbor brought a gift of figs to Aesop's master. Greatly pleased, the master planned to enjoy the figs after his bath and directed that they were put in a cool place until he was ready. While the master was bathing, the overseer and his friends ate the figs. When the master discovered the loss of his figs, the other slaves placed the blame on Aesop. They knew that if Aesop was able to speak, he could defend himself, but they did not fear this stammering slave.   27f   27g   27g

    The master ordered that Aesop be flogged, but Aesop got the master to delay punishment briefly. After drinking a glass of warm water, Aesop ran his fingers down his throat and vomited only water. Pointing at the overseer, he made gestures that the overseer and his friends should do as he did. They drank the water, ran their fingers down their throats—and vomited figs.   27f

    Although Aesop's cleverness saved him from a flogging, it also made an enemy of the overseer. Aesop discovered a basic truth about life: Being right didn't always help one to make friends.   27f

Van Goor and Hacker, *Developmental Exercises for Rules for Writers*, 7th ed. (Boston: Bedford, 2012)

EXERCISE 27-6 ◆ Verb tense and mood

To read about this topic, see sections 27f and 27g in *Rules for Writers*, Seventh Edition.

One sentence in each of the following pairs is correct; the other contains an error in tense or mood. Circle the letters of the correct sentences and edit the incorrect ones. Example:

(a.) **Aesop was sent to work in the farthest field because he had made an enemy of the overseer.**

b. **Maybe the overseer ~~hope~~ _hoped_ Aesop would run away, or maybe he had forgotten that the field was next to a major road.**

1. a. One day a caravan that had lost its way came by the field where Aesop was working.

   b. The caravan driver requested that Aesop shows him the route to Cairo.

2. a. Aesop, who was unable to speak, wanted to have helped him, so he walked with the caravan until it was on the correct road.

   b. Grateful for Aesop's help and wanting to show his appreciation, the caravan leader offered Aesop a reward.

3. a. Aesop silently refused the reward; he had given his help without expecting anything in return.

   b. The caravan leader wanted to leave at once because he lost valuable time on his trip to Cairo.

4. a. When the caravan leader said good-bye, he asked the gods to bless Aesop.

   b. As the caravan moved out of sight, Aesop had decided to take a nap.

5. a. While Aesop slept, the gods restored his speech, proving that good deeds were sometimes rewarded.

   b. When Aesop awoke and could speak, he rejoiced that the gods help those who befriend strangers.

Van Goor and Hacker, *Developmental Exercises for Rules for Writers*, 7th ed. (Boston: Bedford, 2012)

27-6 | Verb tense and mood **89**

EXERCISE 27-7 ◆ Verb tense and mood

To read about this topic, see sections 27f and 27g in *Rules for Writers*, Seventh Edition.

Some of the italicized verbs in the following sentences are correct; others are in the wrong mood. Mark the correct sentences "OK," and change any incorrect verbs. Example:

> **In ancient Greek culture, an overseer usually tried to sell a troublesome slave; if the slave**
>
> ***was* sold, the overseer's life would be easier.**   *OK*

1. When his Greek slave owner ordered that Aesop *be* sold, it was hard to find a buyer for him because he was so ugly.

2. Finally Aesop requested that he *be* allowed to sell himself.

3. Aesop knew that if he *was* not so ugly, many buyers would be glad to get him.

4. If he *was* going to find a buyer, Aesop would need to be clever.

5. One day a caravan that *was* in the slave-trading business stopped at Aesop's master's house.

6. The caravan driver requested that the slave owner *sells* him at least one strong slave.

7. The driver saw that Aesop's muscles *were* strong, but Aesop's hunched back and ugly face discouraged him.

8. Aesop realized that his chances of getting away *were* slim.

9. "If I *was* handsome, I would not be useful as a bogeyman to scare any misbehaving children," he said.

10. If he *were* afraid, the caravan owner did not show it; he laughed at Aesop—and bought him.

Van Goor and Hacker, *Developmental Exercises for Rules for Writers*, 7th ed. (Boston: Bedford, 2012)

EXERCISE 27-8 ◆ Verb tense and mood: Guided review

Correct any errors in verb tense or mood in the following paragraphs. The numbers in the margin refer to relevant rules in sections 27f and 27g of *Rules for Writers*, Seventh Edition. The first revision has been done for you. You should make five more.

     Aesop's death illustrated the implied moral of his last fable: When two enemies

             is
fight each other, it ~~was~~ wise to watch for a larger enemy of both. Aesop's death came   27f

some years after one of his owners gave him his freedom. His former owner would   27f

have liked Aesop to have stayed in the same town, but Aesop became an adviser at the   27f

courts of several kings.

     One of those kings, Croessus, sent Aesop to Delphi to distribute some gifts. The

people of Delphi demanded that he gives them the gifts at once. Aesop refused, having   27g

discovered that the people of Delphi had lied to Croessus about their activities. The

angry people decided that if Aesop was dead, they could distribute the gifts as they   27g

pleased. These people threw Aesop over a cliff to his death, but not before Aesop had

told one more story.

     In the story, a frog invites a rat to dinner. To help the rat across the river to the

frog's house, the frog ties one of the rat's legs to one of his own. Midstream, the frog

tries to drown the rat. The rat puts up such a fight that an eagle flying overhead sees

the commotion and promptly eats both of them.

     "You will succeed in killing me," said Aesop to the people of Delphi, "but a larger

enemy will kill you as well." After Aesop's death, terrible plagues devastated the city.

People believed that the plagues came because of what they did to Aesop. To this day,   27f

the expression "blood of Aesop" refers to an innocent person whose death someone has

avenged.

Van Goor and Hacker, *Developmental Exercises for Rules for Writers*, 7th ed. (Boston: Bedford, 2012)

27-8 | Verb tense and mood: Guided review   **91**

REVIEW OF 19–27 ◆ Grammar

Edit the following paragraphs to eliminate grammatical errors. The numbers in the margin refer to relevant rules in sections 19–27 of *Rules for Writers*, Seventh Edition. First try to find and correct the errors on your own. Then look up the rules if you need to. The first revision has been done for you.

represent
The fables of Aesop ~~represents~~ the Western root of fable, but there are two   21a

strong Eastern roots of fable also: the Panchatantra and the Jataka tales.

The Panchatantra is a collection of stories designed to teach a first prince and

his brothers how to rule over a kingdom. (Until a tutor taught the first prince with

these stories, him and his brothers would never stay in the schoolroom. The boys   24a

listened eagerly to this new tutor who their father had found.) They are usually longer   25a, 23a

than Western fables and have people as well as animals for characters. Their tone

sounds differently, too. Aesop's fables make gentle fun of people's foibles, Panchatantra   26a, 20b

fables teach lessons in how to achieve and hold power. This difference is easily

recognize in the moral to one of the Panchatantra fables: "Do not strike an enemy of   27d

iron with a fist of flesh. Wait until your enemy is stranded at the bottom of a well.

Then throw stones upon him."

The stories that carry the name Jataka tells about the Buddha and the   21a

adventures he had when he came to earth in various incarnations. In these stories, the

Buddha appeared as an animal. Or sometimes simply as a "wise old man." Like the   27f, 19b

Aesop stories, the Jataka tales often depict people's foibles and shortcomings, but the

Jataka tales are not satiric. And they promote compassion rather than power. In one

story, for example, monkeys try to help their friend the gardener by watering newly

planted trees for him. In doing so, they pull each tree out of the ground to see how

long their roots are. Of course the trees die. The Buddha comments, "The ignorant and   22a

foolish, even when they desire to do good, often do ill."

Putting all three traditions of fable together, any reader can choose from a rich

combination of small stories that carry large messages.

Van Goor and Hacker, *Developmental Exercises for Rules for Writers*, 7th ed. (Boston: Bedford, 2012)

EXERCISE 28-1 ◆ ESL verb use: Guided practice

Edit the following paragraphs to correct problems with verbs. The numbers in the margin refer to relevant rules in section 28 of *Rules for Writers*, Seventh Edition. You may need to refer to the list in 27a for the correct form for some irregular verbs. The first revision has been done for you; a suggested revision of this exercise appears in the back of this book.

       come
      Immigrants have ~~came~~ to the United States from all over the world. Initially,   28a

new settlers were mostly European, Irish, or English. By the early twentieth century,

many Asians had took a frightening boat trip across the Pacific to get here. Usually   28a

the men came first. After they had made enough money for passage, their wives and

children were bring over. All thought that if they worked hard, they will make a   28b, 28e

good life, as earlier European immigrants had done. A large number of Chinese and

Japanese settled in the western part of the United States.

      These new immigrants worked on the railroads and in the mines. American

businesses recruited Chinese labor because American workers would not accepted   28c

the wages that were paying. Why did workers decide to come to America anyway?   28b

Somehow the idea got started that America was a "golden mountain" where people

could picked up gold nuggets after an easy climb. Once they got here, most immigrants   28c

worked hard because they hoped making enough money to bring relatives to America   28f

too.

      Before and during World War II, many Germans who had been persecuted

by Hitler escaped to America. After the war, thousands of "displaced persons" were

welcome by the United States. Later, refugees from Asia, Africa, Latin America, and   28b

the Caribbean wanted being accepted. Franklin D. Roosevelt once said, "All of our   28f

people all over the country, except the pure-blooded Indians, are immigrants or

descendants of immigrants." If Roosevelt were alive today, he will know that his   28e

statement is still true.

Van Goor and Hacker, *Developmental Exercises for
Rules for Writers*, 7th ed. (Boston: Bedford, 2012)

28-1 | ESL verb use: Guided practice   **93**

EXERCISE 28-2 ◆ Verb forms

To read about this topic, see section 28a in *Rules for Writers*, Seventh Edition.

Use the tense indicated at the end of each sentence to write the correct form of the verb in brackets. Example:

People from many countries _____*entered*_____ **[*enter*] the United States in the 1980s. [Past]**

1. Eighty percent of the immigrants who _____ [*migrate*] to the United States in the 1980s were Asian or Latin American. [Past]

2. The number of Asians who _____ [*live*] in the United States more than doubled between 1970 and 1980. [Past progressive]

3. People from the Philippines, China, and Korea _____ [*be*] regular immigrants to the United States. [Present perfect]

4. Since 1975, a rush of immigrant refugees _____ [*arrive*] in the United States. [Present perfect progressive]

5. In less than a seven-year period, 600,000 refugees from Vietnam, Laos, and Cambodia _____ [*come*] to the United States. [Past]

Van Goor and Hacker, *Developmental Exercises for Rules for Writers*, 7th ed. (Boston: Bedford, 2012)

EXERCISE 28-3 ◆ Helping verbs, main verbs, and omitted verbs

To read about this topic, see sections 28a to 28d in *Rules for Writers*, Seventh Edition.

A In the following sentences, underline the correct phrase in parentheses. Example:

(Have you hear / <u>Have you heard</u>) of Eckeo Kounlavong?

1. Eckeo Kounlavong (was born / had born) in Laos, lived in a refugee camp in Thailand, and moved to Nashville, Tennessee, in the 1980s.

2. Many people (do not knew / do not know) that in Laos, Eckeo was the leader of the Royal Lao Classical Dancers.

3. Before him, the troupe (had been directed / had been directing) by his father and grandfather.

4. In Laos, the law said that the families of all the dancers (must living / must live) in the palace.

5. They (could to dance / could dance) only for the king and his guests.

B Edit the following sentences for incorrect use of verbs. Put "OK" next to the one correct sentence. Example:

changed
The dancers' lives were ~~change~~ drastically when the Communists gained power in Laos.

6. Eckeo and his mother escaped from Laos to the Nongkhai refugee camp in Thailand.

7. The troupe resettled in Nashville, Tennessee; they been in Nashville ever since.

8. Since 1980, Nashville has attract many Laotians.

9. Nashville has been knowing as the country music capital of the United States.

10. Now Nashville can claims that it is the capital for country music *and* for classical Laotian music.

Van Goor and Hacker, *Developmental Exercises for Rules for Writers*, 7th ed. (Boston: Bedford, 2012)

28-3 | Helping verbs, main verbs, and omitted verbs **95**

EXERCISE 28-4 ◆ Verb forms

To read about this topic, see sections 28a to 28d in *Rules for Writers*, Seventh Edition.

Turn each of the following sentence openings into a complete sentence using the correct form of one of the following: *give, name, take, buy, offer*. Example:

I did not *offer to make coffee.* _____

1. They had been _____

2. He could not _____

3. An award was _____

4. She has already _____

5. They must _____

6. Immigrants have _____

7. Your father has not _____

8. My uncle could _____

9. The house is _____

10. I have been _____

Van Goor and Hacker, *Developmental Exercises for Rules for Writers*, 7th ed. (Boston: Bedford, 2012)

EXERCISE 28-5 ◆ Passive verbs

To read about this topic, see section 28b in *Rules for Writers*, Seventh Edition.

Edit the italicized verb or verb phrase in each of the following sentences to correct the error in the use of helping verbs or main verbs. The revised verbs should all be in the passive voice. You may need to refer to the list in 27a for the correct form for some irregular verbs. Example:

> In the early twentieth century, so many immigrants wanted to enter the United States that
>   *built*
> a special center *was ~~build~~* to process them.
>   ^

1. That center, Ellis Island, *had constructed* to handle five thousand people a day, but often ten thousand people were processed in one day.

2. All immigrants *were check* by a doctor, and an immigrant's coat was marked with a code if the doctor suspected a problem.

3. Everyone knew that if an immigrant *was gave* an "X," the immigrant had practically no chance to enter America; an "X" meant "possible mental problems."

4. Sometimes families were divided because one child was rejected for some reason; often the child *would sent* back alone.

5. Although it was the entrance to a new life for many people, "Ellis Island" *was translate* as "Isle of Tears" in many European languages.

Van Goor and Hacker, *Developmental Exercises for*
Rules for Writers, 7th ed. (Boston: Bedford, 2012)

28-5 | Passive verbs   **97**

EXERCISE 28-6 ◆ Conditional verbs

To read about this topic, see section 28e in *Rules for Writers*, Seventh Edition.

Edit the following paragraph to correct problems with conditional verbs. You may need to refer to the list in 27a for the correct form for some irregular verbs. The first revision has been done for you. You should make five more.

      If my great-grandfather had immigrated today, instead of one hundred years ago, he

probably ~~will~~ *would* have traveled by jet. He came from Croatia to the United States just before the First

World War. In those days, when people left their native country, they usually do so forever. My

great-grandfather missed Croatia, but he liked America very much. He always said that America

was a country where if you work hard, you would be successful. My great-grandfather, who will

be 115 years old if he were alive today, was not as successful as he had hoped. If he has earned

more money, he would have gone back to Croatia to visit. I'm sure my great-grandfather will have

enjoyed that trip if he had ever had the chance to make it.

Van Goor and Hacker, *Developmental Exercises for Rules for Writers*, 7th ed. (Boston: Bedford, 2012)

EXERCISE 28-7 ◆ Verbs followed by gerunds or infinitives

To read about this topic, see section 28f in *Rules for Writers*, Seventh Edition.

The gerunds and infinitives are italicized in the following sentences. Only one in each sentence is correct; correct the other one. Example:

> **Among the many Laotian refugees in Thailand's Nongkhai refugee camp were some**
>
> **members of the Royal Lao Classical Dancers. They wanted ~~*continuing*~~ their** *to continue*
>
> **dancing and discussed *finding* ways that they could stay together.**

1. In the refugee camp in Thailand, the dance troupe began *to think* about *to resettle* together.

2. They enjoyed *to work* together on their music and liked *to perform* for others.

3. Someone suggested *discussing* the idea with resettlement officials who might let them *staying* together.

4. The Laotians wanted *resettling* together; they suggested *sending* the 70 dancers and their families—260 people—to one place.

5. They hardly dared *wishing* for that possibility; nevertheless, they liked *to think* about it.

Van Goor and Hacker, *Developmental Exercises for Rules for Writers,* 7th ed. (Boston: Bedford, 2012)

28-7 | Verbs followed by gerunds or infinitives **99**

EXERCISE 28-8 ◆ Verbs followed by gerunds or infinitives

To read about this topic, see section 28f in *Rules for Writers*, Seventh Edition.

Correct the use of gerunds and infinitives in the following sentences. Put "OK" next to the one correct sentence. Example:

to come

The United States allowed the Laotian dancers ~~coming~~ to America together.

1. The officials let them to bring all their equipment and costumes for performing in their new country.

2. Refugee officials needed to handle thousands of pieces of paper for the dancers before they finished to process them.

3. To avoid splitting up the troupe, officials asked resettlement agencies in America finding sponsors for all of the dancers and their families in one community.

4. People in Nashville, Tennessee, offered to let the troupe settle there.

5. The Laotians wanted thanking the people of Nashville by giving a concert for the city.

Van Goor and Hacker, *Developmental Exercises for Rules for Writers*, 7th ed. (Boston: Bedford, 2012)

EXERCISE 28-9 ◆ ESL verb use: Guided review

Edit the following paragraphs to correct errors in the use of verbs. The numbers in the margin refer to relevant rules in section 28 of *Rules for Writers*, Seventh Edition. The first sentence has been revised for you.

                                            adapted

Although most refugee immigrants have ~~adapt~~ well to life in America, some   **28a**

have not. Many have great difficulty learning English and accepting the customs

of this land they have came to. Other newcomers find that they miss their former   **28a**

homes more than they thought they would. They believe that they would have been

much happier if they have stayed in their native countries. Among the Laotians, the   **28e**

saddest stories indicate that homesickness can even cause death. Would you believe

that homesickness can be so powerful? Young Laotian men with no apparent health

problems have died suddenly in their sleep. Doctors can to give no reason for these   **28c**

deaths, but Laotians believe that the young men wanted going home too much. They   **28f**

say that their bodies died so that their spirits could enjoy to go home again.   **28f**

      Immigrants from Mexico, Cuba, and Puerto Rico have had problems, too. Many

Mexican immigrants been forcibly repatriated because the American government   **28b**

considered them "illegal" immigrants. Most Cuban immigrants in the 1960s expected

their stay in America to be temporary, so they did no become US citizens. Because   **28d**

Puerto Ricans are US citizens, they are not really "immigrants." They are look for a   **28a**

better life, although they do not always find it. So many Puerto Ricans have returned

to their homeland that they have been give a special name, "Neoricans."   **28b**

      Most immigrants, however, have adjust to the new country, changing   **28a**

themselves—and it.

EXERCISE 29-1 ◆ Articles: Guided practice

Edit the following paragraphs to correct the use of articles. The numbers in the margin refer to relevant rules in section 29 of *Rules for Writers*, Seventh Edition. The first revision has been done for you; a suggested revision of this exercise appears in the back of this book.

People all over the world have stories that are part of their culture. Many
                          a
cultures have creation story that explains how the world came to be. Sometimes   29c
story tells how a single piece of the world got its characteristics. It is not surprising   29b
that these stories exist; what is surprising is how similar the stories are. Consider
Cinderella story, for example. Cinderella has different names in different places,   29b
and details of her adventure are not the same; but the basic story echoes around a   29b
world.

In the Egypt, she is called Rhodopis (the word means "rosy cheeked"). Rhodopis   29f
is a Greek slave in a Egyptian home. She does not have eyes or an hair like anyone   29a, 29d
else in the home. Her green eyes look quite different from eyes of the other girls. Their   29b
dark, straight hair almost never gets tangled; her yellow, curly hair blows into tangled   29c
mass around her face. Her light-skinned face turns red and burns when she is in sun   29b
too long. When someone calls her "Rosy Rhodopis," she blushes, and her cheeks become
rosier.

Unable to make the friends with the other girls, Rhodopis turns to the animals   29e
in the nearby woods and streams for companionship.

Van Goor and Hacker, *Developmental Exercises for
Rules for Writers*, 7th ed. (Boston: Bedford, 2012)

EXERCISE 29-2 ◆ Articles

To read about this topic, see section 29 in *Rules for Writers*, Seventh Edition.

Some of the following sentences contain errors in the use of articles. Mark the correct sentences "OK" and correct the others. Example:

> *a*
> Rhodopis charmed the animals: birds, monkeys, and even ~~an~~ hippopotamus would do what
> ^
> she asked.

1. The animals loved to watch her dance; her tiny feet seemed never to touch path.

2. One night when her owner saw her dancing, he was enchanted and decided that such feet deserved special shoes.

3. Rhodopis's shoes had the leather soles, but the toes had a gold on them.

4. When Rhodopis danced, shoes sparkled; they seemed alive.

5. Jealous, the servant girls gave her the more chores; by nighttime, Rhodopis was almost too tired for a single dance.

6. Pharaoh, the ruler of Egypt, sent out a invitation for all his subjects to appear at a court festival.

7. Everyone wanted to go to festival; Rhodopis looked forward to dancing there.

8. The other girls gave her extra chores so that she would not be able to get away: washing the clothes, grinding the grain, and planting the garden.

9. While Rhodopis was doing a laundry, a hippopotamus splashed into the water.

10. The splash muddied Rhodopis's shoes; she cleaned the shoes and set them high on the riverbank to keep them safe.

Van Goor and Hacker, *Developmental Exercises for Rules for Writers*, 7th ed. (Boston: Bedford, 2012)

29-2 | Articles   **103**

EXERCISE 29-3 ◆ Articles

To read about this topic, see section 29 in *Rules for Writers*, Seventh Edition.

Some of the following sentences are missing one article or contain a misused article. Mark the correct sentences "OK" and correct the others. Example:

a

Almost as soon as Rhodopis put her slippers on the bank, huge shadow fell over the land.

^

1. Rhodopis looked up and saw an huge falcon flying overhead.

2. Rhodopis bowed her head, recognizing the falcon as a symbol of great god Horus.

3. She greeted the bird politely; but when bird flew away, he took one of her slippers with him.

4. Tearful, Rhodopis tucked the other slipper into her tunic and resumed a work.

5. She tried to imagine dancing on one foot; idea made her laugh.

6. The bird flew to Memphis, went to the festival, and found the Pharaoh, Amasis.

7. Amasis sat on his throne, immobilized by a boredom; then the bird dropped the shoe into his lap.

8. Amasis recognized Horus in the falcon and decided that the shoe was a sign to tell him whom he should marry.

9. Amasis got into his chariot to look all through Egypt for owner of the shoe, who he knew would be his bride.

10. All of people went home from the festival, including the servant girls who had left Rhodopis at home.

Van Goor and Hacker, *Developmental Exercises for Rules for Writers*, 7th ed. (Boston: Bedford, 2012)

EXERCISE 29-4 ◆ Articles: Guided review

Edit the following paragraphs to correct the use of articles. The numbers in the margin refer to relevant rules in section 29 of *Rules for Writers*, Seventh Edition. The first revision has been done for you.

Pharaoh Amasis traveled all over ~~the~~ Egypt searching for his bride-to-be. The   29f

search took the very long time. Everywhere, beautiful women came to put their feet   29c

into a rose-gold slipper he carried with him. Not one of them could fit her foot into so   29b

small a shoe.

When Amasis had not found the owner of the shoe in his own land, he decided

to look along Nile River. His boats were brightly decorated, and musicians made an   29f, 29a

loud noise of trumpets and gongs as they traveled. The noise attracted many people

to river, but Rhodopis was so frightened that she ran to hide in a weed patch. Amasis   29b

stopped his boat so that the people along the shore could reach him and pay an   29d

attention to his words.

When Amasis held out the slipper, all of the servant girls made effort to put it   29c

on; it fit no one. Then Amasis saw Rhodopis in weeds and ordered her to try it on also.   29b

The shoe fit, and Rhodopis pulled its mate out of her tunic.

Wearing both slippers, Rhodopis joined Amasis on a boat. Rhodopis was on her   29b

way to an happy life as the new queen of Egypt.   29a

Van Goor and Hacker, *Developmental Exercises for Rules for Writers*, 7th ed. (Boston: Bedford, 2012)

29-4 | Articles: Guided review **105**

EXERCISE 30/31-1 ✦ Sentence structure, prepositions, and idiomatic expressions: Guided practice

Edit the following paragraphs to correct any misuses of subjects, repetitions, adverbs, adjectives, participles, and prepositions. The numbers in the margin refer to relevant rules in sections 30 and 31 of *Rules for Writers*, Seventh Edition. The first revision has been done for you; a suggested revision of this exercise appears in the back of this book.

A descendant of one of the earliest immigrants ~~at~~ *to* North America played a   31a

pivotal role in helping later Americans explore their country. Were tribes of American   30b

Indians living all over what is now the United States. Each tribe had its own language

and customs. Some tribes raided others and took prisoners who then became the

raiding tribes' slaves. That is what happened to a young Shoshone girl now known as

Sacagawea.

This girl, like many young girls, she had a nickname, "He-toe." "He-toe" was the   30c

sound a local bird made, and the girl's movements were as swift as that bird's. When a

raiding party of Hidatsas captured easily this young girl, they named her Sacagawea—   30f

"bird woman." Sacagawea was about twelve years old. The frightening young girl did   30g

not try to escape but accepted her role and worked for her captors. At a few months,   31a

she had acquired a reputation for good sense and good work.

The tribe married Sacagawea to a white man, Toussaint Charbonneau; she was

his second wife. Soon pregnant, this typical Indian wife she did the chores and left all   30c

decisions to her husband; but inwardly, she longed to explore new places and meet new

people. She may have been controlling by her husband, but she never missed a chance   30g

to learn whatever she could.

When white men appeared, many Indians were curious. Sacagawea had never

seen a man with yellow hair—or red hair. Nor had she ever seen a black man. All

these men were trying to get to the "Big Water" far to the west. They would have to

cross mountains that they had not even seen them yet. They needed horses and guides   30d

that the Shoshone could supply and an interpreter who could speak the Shoshone

language. Imagine their surprise when this interpreter, whom they had hoped to find

him, turned out to be a woman—a Shoshone young attractive woman.   30d, 30h

106   30/31-1 | Sentence structure, prepositions, and idiomatic expressions: Guided practice

Van Goor and Hacker, Developmental Exercises for Rules for Writers, 7th ed. (Boston: Bedford, 2012)

EXERCISE 30/31-2 ◆ Omissions and needless repetitions

To read about this topic, see sections 30b to 30d in *Rules for Writers*, Seventh Edition.

In the following sentences, add needed subjects or expletives and delete any repeated subjects, objects, or adverbs. Mark the two correct sentences "OK." Example:

> **The white men who came ashore ~~they~~ had been sent by the Great White Father in**
>
> **Washington to blaze a trail to the Big Water.**

1. The two leaders among the white men they were Meriwether Lewis and William Clark.

2. Clark's red beard and hair puzzled Sacagawea; was hard to believe that those red hairs were real.

3. Sacagawea also watched in amazement as York, the black man, he washed his hands and face and none of his color came off.

4. The men quickly began building the shelters that they were going to live in them.

5. Was a lot of noise as they felled trees and fitted the logs together to build cabins.

6. The white men hired Charbonneau as an interpreter (he spoke both Hidatsa and French) and told him to bring Sacagawea along too.

7. Sacagawea could hardly believe that she would see her own people again in the place where she had lived there before.

8. Charbonneau and Sacagawea, who was now near the end of her pregnancy, were given a cabin to live in that winter.

9. Sacagawea's friends came often to the house that she was staying in it, usually asking for medical help while they were there.

10. Sacagawea, who learned how to cook for the white men, she tried especially to please Captain Clark, who gave her an English name, Janie.

Van Goor and Hacker, *Developmental Exercises for Rules for Writers*, 7th ed. (Boston: Bedford, 2012)

30/31-2 | Omissions and needless repetitions   **107**

EXERCISE 30/31-3 ◆ Present and past participles

To read about this topic, see section 30g in *Rules for Writers*, Seventh Edition.

Circle the letter of the sentence that answers the question. Example:

In which sentence were the men eager to get started?

a.   **By April, the snows were melting and the men in the camp were exciting to begin moving on.**

(b.)   **By April, the snows were melting and the men in the camp were excited to begin moving on.**

1.   In which sentence were the men happy?

    a.   Sacagawea always found the men pleasing.

    b.   Sacagawea always found the men pleased.

2.   In which sentence was Sacagawea eager to get to the mountains?

    a.   As they neared the mountains, where the Shoshone lived, Sacagawea grew more and more excited.

    b.   As they neared the mountains, where the Shoshone lived, Sacagawea grew more and more exciting.

3.   In which sentence did Clark enjoy watching Sacagawea?

    a.   Watching Sacagawea bargain for horses, Clark was fascinating.

    b.   Watching Sacagawea bargain for horses, Clark was fascinated.

4.   In which sentence were the travelers unhappy?

    a.   For the four months they stayed on the West Coast, the travelers had only twelve days without rain; all of them found this weather depressed.

    b.   For the four months they stayed on the West Coast, the travelers had only twelve days without rain; all of them found this weather depressing.

5.   In which sentence did the decision make everyone fearful?

    a.   On the way home, Lewis and Clark made a frightened decision to divide the crew and send the men along different trails.

    b.   On the way home, Lewis and Clark made a frightening decision to divide the crew and send the men along different trails.

Van Goor and Hacker, *Developmental Exercises for Rules for Writers*, 7th ed. (Boston: Bedford, 2012)

EXERCISE 30/31-4 ◆ Placement of adjectives

To read about this topic, see section 30h in *Rules for Writers*, Seventh Edition.

Insert the given adjectives in their correct positions in the following sentences. Do not add commas. Example:

> **old, experienced**
>
> *Experienced* _____*old*_____ women came to help Sacagawea when it was time for her baby to be born.

1. log, warm

   Sacagawea was glad that she was living in a _____ _____ cabin when birthing time came.

2. hard, labor

   The baby did not come easily. Neither the old women's skill nor Captain Clark's medicines did much to ease Sacagawea's _____ _____ pains.

3. the, old, bell-shaped

   Finally, one of the men said that swallowing some rattles (_____ _____ _____ scales on a rattlesnake's tail) often brought a quick and easy birth.

4. dark, strange, this

   Captain Clark had collected some rattles; he crushed two of them and added some water. One of the old women gave _____ _____ _____ potion to Sacagawea.

5. male, a, healthy

   Ten minutes later, Jean Baptiste Charbonneau arrived—_____ _____ _____ child who would be affectionately called "Pomp," the Shoshone word for "firstborn."

Van Goor and Hacker, *Developmental Exercises for Rules for Writers*, 7th ed. (Boston: Bedford, 2012)

30/31-4 | Placement of adjectives   **109**

EXERCISE 30/31-5 ◆ Sentence structure, prepositions, and idiomatic expressions: Guided review

Edit the following paragraphs to correct any misuses of subjects, repetitions, adverbs, adjectives, participles, and prepositions. Do not change correct sentences. The numbers in the margin refer to relevant rules in sections 30 and 31 of *Rules for Writers*, Seventh Edition. The first revision has been done for you.

By the time Lewis and Clark ~~found~~ finally the Pacific Ocean and made their way   30f

home again, Sacagawea not only had gotten her wish to travel but also had become a

favorite of all the crew. Had served as interpreter, guide, cook, nurse, and mother for   30b

everyone who needed her. She and Pomp seemed like family to Clark and his men.

When Captain Clark left, he offered to take Pomp (now almost two) to St.

Louis and educate him. Sacagawea said, "Not now," but later the whole family moved

in St. Louis. No one is sure what happened next. Most historians agree that after   31a

a few months Charbonneau left gladly St. Louis "with his wife" and spent time at   30f

a new fort, Fort Manuel. There his wife she sickened and died of a fever in 1812.   30c

Since Charbonneau had several Shoshone wives, cannot be sure that this wife was   30b

Sacagawea. Historical records show that Clark became the legal guardian for Pomp

and his baby sister the year that Charbonneau's wife died.

Pomp stayed with Captain Clark. At nineteen, he met a German rich prince who   30h

was touring America and went to Europe with him for six years. Later this mountain

man, whose mother had trekked with him halfway across the continent before he

could walk, he returned to mountain life for good, working as a trader, a hunter, and   30c

an interpreter.

The Shoshone oral tradition says that Sacagawea quarreled with Charbonneau

and left him, stayed for a while with the Comanches, met up with her son and a

nephew, and ended up at the Wind River Reservation in Wyoming, where she died on

April 4, 1884, almost one hundred years old. The Wyoming branch of the Daughters of

the American Revolution were convincing that the oral tradition was true and erected   30g

a memorial stone there.

30/31-5 | Sentence structure, prepositions, and idiomatic
expressions: Guided review

110

Van Goor and Hacker, *Developmental Exercises for Rules for Writers,* 7th ed. (Boston: Bedford, 2012)

No other American woman has had so many memorials dedicated to her. Among

them are historical markers, lakes, a river, a mountain peak, and a park. On 1999, the   31a

United States even honored her on its new dollar—a gold-colored coin. Just below the

word *Liberty* on that coin is a likeness of Sacagawea with her infant son. Now travel-

loving Sacagawea can go wherever that dollar goes there.   30d

Van Goor and Hacker, *Developmental Exercises for
Rules for Writers*, 7th ed. (Boston: Bedford, 2012)

30/31-5 | Sentence structure, prepositions, and idiomatic
expressions: Guided review   **111**

REVIEW OF 28–31 ◆ Multilingual Writers and ESL Challenges

This paragraph has eleven errors. The numbers in the margin refer to relevant rules in sections 28–31 of *Rules for Writers*, Seventh Edition. You may need to refer to the list in 27a for the correct form for some irregular verbs. The first revision has been done for you. Find and correct ten more errors.

       given
  Immigrants have ~~gave~~ the United States their languages, their foods, and   28a

their customs. Many people are not aware for all the cultural influences. Native   31c

Americans gave the United States the names for half of its states. *Texas* is a

Native American old word for "friends," and *Idaho* means "good morning." Spanish   30h

immigrants gave the United States the longest name for any of its cities. In Spanish,

is *El Pueblo de Nuestra Señora la Reina de los Angeles de Porciúncula* — Los Angeles.   30b

American cuisine now includes foods from many other traditions, from Chinese

sweet-and-sour pork to Greek baklava. American children who enjoy to eat pizza or   28f

spaghetti or tacos think they are eating American food. Since the Germans brought

the Christmas tree to America, every immigrant group that celebrates Christmas

it has added something to American Christmas customs. Fiestas and serenades are   30c

common in the United States, and even New England children often want to break

open a piñata on their birthday parties. Every summer in Washington, DC, Americans   31a

celebrate the diversity of their culture with an excited folk festival. Groups from   30g

many different cultures in America bring an equipment to produce their own foods   29e

and festivities on the national Mall, where many other Americans can enjoy them. A   29a

alien visitor would not be able to tell which songs and stories are "American," for the

food, festivals, dances, music, and folktales of immigrant groups have became part of   28a

America's own culture.

Van Goor and Hacker, *Developmental Exercises for Rules for Writers*, 7th ed. (Boston: Bedford, 2012)

EXERCISE 32/33-1 ◆ The comma and unnecessary commas: Guided practice

Edit the following essay by adding commas where they are needed and removing unnecessary commas. The numbers in the margin refer to relevant rules in sections 32 and 33 of *Rules for Writers*, Seventh Edition. The first revision has been done for you; answers to this exercise appear in the back of this book.

If a boy wanted to join the football team at Carlisle Indian School, he had to   32b

go through a difficult test. Any boy who wanted to be on the team had to stand at one

of the goal lines; all the first-string players stood around the field. When the ball was

punted to the new boy, he had to catch it and try to get all the way to the other end

zone with it. The team members tried to stop him before he could get very far. Only a

few players had ever gotten as far as the fifty-yard line so "Pop" Warner, coach at the   32a

Carlisle Indian School considered it a good test.   32e

One day a quiet Native American boy surprised Pop. The boy caught the ball,

started running, wheeled away from the first players who tried to stop him, shook

off the others and ran the ball all the way to the opposite goal line. Convinced that   32c

the player's success was an accident, the coach ordered him to run the play again.

Brusquely, the coach spoke to the players, and reminded them that this workout was   33a

supposed to be tackling practice. Jim, the nineteen-year-old six-footer, simply said   32h

"Nobody tackles Jim." Then he ran the ball to the goal line a second time.

Well, almost no one tackled Jim Thorpe successfully for many years. Life itself

got him down and made him fumble more often than his football opponents did, but,   33h

he was usually able to recover and go on. The first blow was the death of his twin

brother while the two boys were still in grade school. This tragedy was followed by

others; by the time Jim was twenty-five, his mother and his father had also died.

They left him a Native American heritage: His father was half Irish and half Native

American and his mother was the granddaughter of a famous, Native American   32a, 33d

warrior named Chief Black Hawk.

Fortunately or unfortunately, along with his Native American heritage came great pride and stoicism. That pride kept him silent when the greatest blow of all came: He was forced to return the Olympic medals he had won in 1912 because he was declared to be not an amateur. He dealt stoically with his personal tragedies. When infantile paralysis struck his son Jim Thorpe disappeared for a few days to deal with the tragedy alone. His stoicism also saw him through a demotion to the minor leagues and sad years of unemployment and poverty before his death.   32b

Even death's tackle may not have been totally successful: After Jim Thorpe's death his Olympic medals were returned, and a town was named after him.   32b

Van Goor and Hacker, *Developmental Exercises for Rules for Writers,* 7th ed. (Boston: Bedford, 2012)

EXERCISE 32/33-2 ◆ The comma

To read about this topic, see sections 32 and 33 in *Rules for Writers*, Seventh Edition.

A Insert commas where they are needed with coordinating conjunctions in the following sentences. If a sentence is correct, mark it "OK." Example:

Coach Warner was impressed with the new player's skill, and he looked for a chance
                                                                     ^

to try him in an actual game.

1. Jim passed Coach Warner's test but he did not get to play right away.

2. Then in one game a player was injured and Coach Warner sent Jim in.

3. At first, no one but Jim and the coach believed that Jim could play well enough.

4. He lost five yards the first time he got the ball but the next time he ran sixty-five yards for a touchdown.

5. His sports career began with that game and included major honors in track, lacrosse, baseball, and football.

B Insert commas where they are needed after an introductory element, in a series, and with coordinate adjectives. If a sentence is correct, mark it "OK." Example:

After trying to tackle Thorpe only once, Jim's most famous opponent never played
                                          ^

football again.

6. In a game against Army, Thorpe had the ball.

7. One Army player tried to tackle Jim, failed, injured his knee in the process and had to be helped from the field.

8. That strong confident player said in later years, "Thorpe gained ground; he always gained ground."

9. Although the injured player was never able to play football again he became famous in other ways.

10. He became supreme commander of the Allied armies in Europe in World War II and thirty-fourth president of the United States—Dwight D. Eisenhower.

Van Goor and Hacker, *Developmental Exercises for Rules for Writers*, 7th ed. (Boston: Bedford, 2012)

32/33-2 | The comma   **115**

EXERCISE 32/33-3 ◆ The comma

To read about this topic, see sections 32 and 33 in *Rules for Writers*, Seventh Edition.

A Add commas where they are needed around nonrestrictive elements. If a sentence is correct, mark it "OK." Example:

Jim Thorpe's Olympic medals, which he won in 1912 but had to forfeit, were for the
                          ^   ^
pentathlon and the decathlon. [Thorpe won Olympic medals only in 1912.]

1. The Carlisle students who needed summer jobs often played baseball for Carolina teams. [Not all Carlisle students needed summer jobs.]

2. The players who were willing to lie used false names when they played for little-known teams; Jim did not. [Only some of the players were willing to lie.]

3. Those who had received money for playing their sport were disqualified because they were no longer "amateurs." [Only some received money.]

4. The five-sport event which is called the pentathlon is difficult. [There is only one five-sport event.]

5. The decathlon which is a ten-sport event is considered the most difficult of all Olympic events. [There is only one ten-sport event.]

B Add commas as necessary in the following sentences. Example:

In Stockholm, Sweden's King Gustav presented the 1912 Olympic winners with their gold
            ^
medals; in addition, he spoke briefly to some of them.
                    ^

6. As King Gustav presented Jim Thorpe's 1912 Olympic medal, he said to Jim "Sir you are the greatest athlete in the world."

7. In January 1913 however a newspaper reported that Jim had been paid for playing for the Carolina baseball teams.

8. When the Amateur Athletic Union (AAU) asked Jim said he had been paid.

9. Stating that he had not known he was doing wrong, Jim insisted that he had acted no worse than athletes who used false names.

10. After Jim presented his case, the AAU made its ruling; specifically it ruled that Jim had not been an amateur at the time of his participation in the Olympics.

Van Goor and Hacker, *Developmental Exercises for Rules for Writers*, 7th ed. (Boston: Bedford, 2012)

EXERCISE 32/33-4 ◆ The comma

To read about this topic, see sections 32 and 33 in *Rules for Writers*, Seventh Edition.

Edit the following paragraphs to correct the use of commas. The first revision has been done for you. You should add ten more commas.

When the Amateur Athletic Union ruled that 1912 Olympic winner Jim Thorpe had not been an amateur at the time he won his medals, several consequences followed. Once the ruling was formally stated, Jim Thorpe's name was erased from the Olympic records. In addition he had to return his medals. Friends wanted him to fight the AAU ruling but he was too proud to do so.

During the next sixteen years that Jim played football was quite different from what it is today. Players then had no league, no formal schedule, no helmet requirements and often no salaries. Then representatives of eight concerned teams met to form a league. The organization they formed which was called the American Professional Football Association later became the National Football League; Jim Thorpe was its first president.

Jim's playing declined with the years until on November 30, 1929 an Associated Press story described him as "a mere shadow of his former self." No longer able to play sports Thorpe had to dig ditches during the Depression years. When the 1932 Olympics were held in Los Angeles California he could not afford to buy a ticket.

Van Goor and Hacker, *Developmental Exercises for Rules for Writers*, 7th ed. (Boston: Bedford, 2012)

32/33-4 | The comma **117**

EXERCISE 32/33-5 ◆ Unnecessary commas

To read about this topic, see sections 32 and 33 in *Rules for Writers*, Seventh Edition.

Each of the following sentences contains one unnecessary comma. Delete the comma that is not needed. Example:

> **Along with other bad news about Thorpe, newspaper stories reported/that he drank too much and that drinking caused his second marriage to go wrong.**

1. After Jim Thorpe's death, his friends worked to have his medals restored, and to get his name back on the list of Olympic winners.

2. Knowing that they would not be happy, until the AAU and the Olympic committees changed their minds, his friends made repeated appeals.

3. The AAU acted first, reversing its position some years later, (in 1973) by saying that Thorpe's titles should be restored.

4. The American Olympic Committee agreed two years later, but, it was not until 1982 that the International Olympic Committee voted to restore Jim's titles.

5. New, Olympic medals were presented to Thorpe's children in a 1983 ceremony in Los Angeles, California.

6. However, the International Olympic Committee, did not erase the names of the second-place finishers.

7. Even though Thorpe had beaten the other "winners," his friends had to accept the fact, that Jim would be listed only as a cochampion.

8. In the hearts of Jim's supporters remains the honest, firm conviction, that Jim should be listed as the sole winner of each of the races he won.

9. They thought that the International Olympic Committee's reversing its position, restoring the titles, and awarding Thorpe's medals to his children, were not enough.

10. It is not likely that there will be any further action, such as, erasing the other winners' names.

Van Goor and Hacker, *Developmental Exercises for Rules for Writers*, 7th ed. (Boston: Bedford, 2012)

EXERCISE 32/33-6 ◆ Unnecessary commas

To read about this topic, see sections 32 and 33 in *Rules for Writers*, Seventh Edition.

One sentence in each of the following pairs is correctly punctuated. Circle the letter of the correct sentence and edit the incorrect sentence. Example:

a. **Jim Thorpe was a greater athlete than any other athlete of his time.**

b. **In 1950, an Associated Press poll of hundreds of sportswriters indicated that Thorpe was better/than any other athlete from 1900 to 1950.**

1. a. According to many experts, (sportswriters, coaches, and the like), Thorpe would always be considered the best athlete of his era.

   b. Others predicted that modern knowledge of various aspects of training (nutrition, exercise, and the like) would produce even greater players than Thorpe.

2. a. People said, that Thorpe's confidence in himself was so great that he often skipped practice at the Olympics, and they told the "broad jump story" to illustrate his confidence.

   b. Observers said that he measured the broad jump distance with his eye, decided he could jump it, and lay down in a hammock for a nap, not even bothering to take a practice run at it.

3. a. In his 289 games in baseball's major leagues, the only statistic that suggested trouble was his batting average of .252.

   b. It seems that the only thing that really bothered Jim, was hitting curveballs.

4. a. He had a peculiar style of running, that left his football tacklers flat on the ground.

   b. He would twist his hips away from the player who was after him.

5. a. He would wait until that player's head was at the exact, dangerous, height.

   b. Then he would swing his hips with full, direct force right into the player's head.

Van Goor and Hacker, *Developmental Exercises for Rules for Writers*, 7th ed. (Boston: Bedford, 2012)

32/33-6 | Unnecessary commas   **119**

EXERCISE 32/33-7 ◆ The comma and unnecessary commas: Guided review

Edit the following paragraphs by adding commas where they are needed and removing commas where they are not needed. The numbers in the margin refer to relevant rules in sections 32 and 33 of *Rules for Writers*, Seventh Edition. The first revision has been done for you.

Quarrels about one of America's greatest athletes, Jim Thorpe, continue. Even though the decision about his Olympic standing has been made, other quarrels about him remain.   32b

After Jim Thorpe died his wife had to choose a burial place. Everyone assumed   32b
he would be buried in his home state of Oklahoma, but, his wife made other   33h
arrangements. Some people from Mauch Chunk, Pennsylvania, made her an offer.
They said, that they wanted Jim buried in their town. Having his body there would   33h
make more tourists want to come to their small, Pennsylvania town. They talked of a   33d
burial place, a Jim Thorpe Museum and a hospital in his memory. They also offered to   32c
change the name of the town from Mauch Chunk to Jim Thorpe.

Mrs. Thorpe, who wanted a memorial for Jim, agreed to these proposals, and   33a
gave Jim's body to the town. It is probable that at the core of her decision was the
desire for Jim Thorpe to be remembered. After some negotiation, the agreement was
concluded and the town is now on the map as "Jim Thorpe."   32a

Jim's wife, not his children, made the agreement. His children, seven sons
and daughters, wanted his body buried in Oklahoma. They wanted the body to be
given a traditional Native American burial. They wanted the town to give back their
father's body. Jack Thorpe, one of the sons, said to a *Sports Illustrated* writer in 1982   32h
"Dad's spirit is still roaming." In Jim Thorpe's family pride is still part of the Thorpe   32b
heritage. The family has not given up the struggle. Other people have also asked the
townspeople to change their minds.

Jim Thorpe lived a tough, honest, gifted, and controversial, life. Even if his   33c
records are someday broken, he will remain a legend of the American sports world.

Van Goor and Hacker, *Developmental Exercises for Rules for Writers*, 7th ed. (Boston: Bedford, 2012)

EXERCISE 34-1 ◆ The semicolon: Guided practice

Edit the following paragraphs to correct problems with the use of semicolons. The numbers in the margin refer to relevant rules in section 34 of *Rules for Writers*, Seventh Edition. The first revision has been done for you; answers to this exercise appear in the back of this book.

When Cheryl Toussaint came in second in a race she had never planned to run; she started on a road that led to the Olympics and a world record.　　　　34d

Cheryl began running almost by accident one day when she went to watch a city-sponsored track meet in Brooklyn, New York. During the preliminaries, the officials announced an "open" race, it was one that anyone could enter. Cheryl wanted　　34a
to enter; but she was dressed in a skirt and sandals. Four things made her run; one　　34d, 34d
friend traded shoes with her, another let her borrow jeans, several called her "chicken" if she didn't run, and one girl dared her to run. Coming in second in that race led this teenager to many places, including Munich, Germany, Toronto, Canada, and Montreal,　　34c
Canada.

There were, however, many races to run and lessons to learn. Cheryl joined the all-female Atoms Track Club, and she began training under Coach Fred Thompson. Like most coaches, Fred had his own way of testing newcomers. He watched new runners carefully, however, he gave them no special attention. Instead, he just gave　　34b
them orders one after another. He would tell Cheryl to run laps, perform exercises, and repeat practice starts, at the same time, he would never comment on how she　　34a
performed. If the newcomers endured the hard, time-consuming workouts without encouragement or praise; Thompson was sure that they were ready for real coaching.　　34d

Cheryl quit after two months, for six more months, she stayed away from the　　34a
club. During that time, she thought about her attitude toward work, her poor record at school, her pleasure in running, and her lack of goals. When she returned to the club;　　34d
Thompson welcomed her back. Coach Thompson knew how special Cheryl was, he not　　34a
only convinced her she was college material but also pushed her to achieve the highest goal of the amateur athlete—competing in the Olympics.

EXERCISE 34-2 ◆ The semicolon

To read about this topic, see section 34 in *Rules for Writers*, Seventh Edition.

Add semicolons in the five word groups that need them; mark the other word groups "OK." Example:

> **Cheryl Toussaint's first official run was an indication of her character and determination;
> no one could find fault with her effort.**

1. Cheryl's first official run—at a cross-country meet on Long Island—would certainly have impressed any coach every person watching was astounded by her perseverance.

2. Coach Thompson had warned her not to start too fast but to stay with the pack. "Just try to finish," he said.

3. Too excited to follow his directions, Cheryl took off at top speed at the starting gun, moreover, she did not slow down even after she was a hundred yards in front of everyone else.

4. Cheryl kept that distance for most of the run, she did not allow herself any slack.

5. Then, with only a hundred yards to go, Cheryl gave out, she collapsed and fell down.

6. Immediately, she got to her knees and started crawling. She crawled toward the finish line, not toward the grassy area where runners who left the race were supposed to go.

7. She stood up, staggered a little farther, and fell again. Once more she started crawling.

8. Not able to get to her feet again, Cheryl continued to crawl, after all, she was nearly at the finish line.

9. She had almost reached the finish line when another runner passed her and won the race.

10. "I knew at that moment," said her coach, "that this girl was going to be something special." Her coach was right.

Van Goor and Hacker, *Developmental Exercises for Rules for Writers*, 7th ed. (Boston: Bedford, 2012)

EXERCISE 34-3 ◆ The semicolon

To read about this topic, see section 34 in *Rules for Writers*, Seventh Edition.

Each of the following sentences contains two semicolons but should have only one. Delete the incorrect one and replace it with other punctuation if necessary. Example:

> **No one else had ever seen anything special in Cheryl, who had never shown any ambition; her teachers had labeled her a "slow learner" long before she got to high school.**

1. Cheryl had to beg her teachers to allow her to take college preparatory courses; they were sure she would fail; no matter how hard she tried.

2. Coach Thompson did many things for Cheryl; including coaching track, prodding her about schoolwork, encouraging good eating habits, and insisting that she think about college; most important of all, he gave her faith in herself.

3. All of the runners knew that if they made qualifying times; Coach Thompson would see to it that they were entered in the national meets; however, they also knew that if they did not qualify, they were off the team.

4. Cheryl soon discovered that she had to schedule her time; or she would fail at school or at track or at both; thinking about Coach Thompson, she began to care.

5. By the time Cheryl graduated from high school, she was an A student; this "slow learner" received an academic scholarship to New York University; although she had once thought only an athletic scholarship was possible.

Van Goor and Hacker, *Developmental Exercises for Rules for Writers*, 7th ed. (Boston: Bedford, 2012)

34-3 | The semicolon   **123**

EXERCISE 34-4 ◆ The semicolon: Guided review

Edit the following paragraphs to correct problems with the use of semicolons. The numbers in the margin refer to relevant rules in section 34 of *Rules for Writers*, Seventh Edition. The first revision has been done for you.

Every runner dreams of winning both individual and relay medals at the

Olympics,/; in 1972, Cheryl Toussaint was no exception. When she did not qualify   34a

for the individual 800-meter finals; she pinned her hopes on the relay race. Her   34d

teammates on the American team were ready: Mabel Ferguson, Madeline Jackson, and

Kathy Hammond. The relay was Cheryl's last chance to win a medal, unfortunately, it   34b

seemed that everything was against her.

Cheryl began the third leg of the qualifying heat with runners ahead of her.

Then a runner in front of her fell. As Cheryl dashed around her, another runner

stepped on the heel of Cheryl's left shoe, so Cheryl was running with her shoe half on

and half off. She needed to stop and pull the shoe on, but she knew two things: She

would lose valuable time, and this was her team's last chance to qualify for the finals.

She kept running, very soon the shoe flew up in the air. Cheryl wondered whether   34a

the shoe would hit anyone, whether TV viewers could see her bare foot, and whether

people in the stands had noticed. But she ran on, passing the other runners. Her

team qualified for the finals that day, and in the finals Cheryl and her teammates won

silver medals.

Cheryl remembered her very first run in Brooklyn, in which she hadn't even

known how to start, her first "real" race, in which she'd crawled to the finish line, and   34c

the Olympic 800-meter individual run in which she'd failed to qualify. She could laugh

about all those memories now, for she and her teammates were Olympic medalists.

Back home, Cheryl kept to her plans: graduating from college (with a B+

average), getting a job in the Federal Reserve Bank's management training program,

and training for the next Olympics. She knew that nothing would ever mean as much

to her again as track, the Atoms, and Coach Thompson had meant her success was   34a

also theirs.

Van Goor and Hacker, *Developmental Exercises for Rules for Writers*, 7th ed. (Boston: Bedford, 2012)

EXERCISE 35-1 ◆ The colon: Guided practice

In the following paragraph, insert colons where they are needed and delete any improperly used colons. The numbers in the margin refer to relevant rules in section 35 of *Rules for Writers*, Seventh Edition. The first revision has been done for you; answers to this exercise appear in the back of this book.

In 1951, Althea Gibson broke the color barrier in women's tennis and became admired all over the world. No one who knew her as a teenager would have predicted her success. By the time Althea Gibson reached her teens, her record showed three indications of trouble/: running away from home, dropping out of school, and losing   **35a** the one job she had been able to find. To survive in her neighborhood, Althea depended on: a small welfare allowance, occasional handouts, and plain old luck. She listed   **35d** her skills as the following, good bowler, great two-on-two basketball player, and fast   **35a** paddleball player. Even after she began playing tennis and moving in upper-class Harlem society, she resented the efforts of the society ladies to improve her. They busied themselves with tasks such as: correcting her manners and restricting her   **35d** behavior. Looking back, she summed up her earlier attitude she said she hadn't been   **35a** ready to study about "how to be a fine lady." At eighteen, she finally got: a waitressing   **35d** job, a congenial roommate, and a good friend.

Van Goor and Hacker, *Developmental Exercises for Rules for Writers*, 7th ed. (Boston: Bedford, 2012)

35-1 | The colon: Guided practice   **125**

EXERCISE 35-2 ◆ The colon

To read about this topic, see section 35 in *Rules for Writers*, Seventh Edition.

In the following sentences, insert colons where they can be effectively used. Example:

> **In 1957, Althea Gibson won the women's title at the most prestigious tennis tournament in the world: Wimbledon.**
> ^

1. Althea Gibson broke the color barrier in women's tennis she was the first black female player to compete in national championships.

2. Two tennis-playing doctors opened their homes to her so she could finish high school and go to college Dr. Hubert A. Eaton of Wilmington, North Carolina, and Dr. Robert W. Johnson of Lynchburg, Virginia.

3. Her life in a southern high school was not pleasant; if she had written a book about it, she could have titled it *Misfit, A Yankee Woman in a Southern School*.

4. Besides tennis, Althea's other love was music the drums, the chorus, and especially the saxophone.

5. Her friend Sugar Ray Robinson firmly advised her to go to college "No matter what you want to do, tennis or music or what, you'll be better at it if you get some education."

Van Goor and Hacker, *Developmental Exercises for Rules for Writers*, 7th ed. (Boston: Bedford, 2012)

EXERCISE 35-3 ◆ The colon

To read about this topic, see section 35 in *Rules for Writers*, Seventh Edition.

In the following paragraphs, the italicized words indicate where two parts of a sentence come together. Decide whether the sentence needs a colon to join these parts. If it does, insert one. If it does not, mark the spot "OK." The first sentence has been marked for you. Hint: You will need very few colons.

OK

Althea Gibson began playing *tennis when* she was a young teenager in the 1940s. In just over a decade, she *became one* of the world's greatest women tennis players.

The tennis world began to notice her after only a few years of amateur *play she* was winning women's singles meets one after the other. In 1950 and the years immediately *following, she* became more and more famous. By 1957, Althea Gibson, the rising young tennis star, was well known on both sides of the *Atlantic she* was the most respected woman player in Britain and America. In both countries, she won the national women's singles title two years in a row: 1957 and 1958. The British meet, which is *called Wimbledon,* is generally regarded *as the* unofficial world championship meet. Gibson also played on the US team at other major meets, *including the* Wightman Cup meet. That meet is a special British-American *meet that* pits US women against British women. When Althea Gibson was on the US team, the United States won.

Gibson's retirement from tennis in 1958 *was a* complete surprise to her fans. What reason did she give for her retirement? She had *decided to* become a professional golfer!

Van Goor and Hacker, *Developmental Exercises for Rules for Writers,* 7th ed. (Boston: Bedford, 2012)

35-3 | The colon **127**

EXERCISE 35-4 ◆ The colon: Guided review

In the following paragraph, insert colons where they are needed and delete any improperly used colons. The numbers in the margin refer to relevant rules in section 35 of *Rules for Writers*, Seventh Edition. The first revision has been done for you.

When the Eatons of North Carolina invited Althea Gibson to move into their

home for the school year, she hesitated. Northerner Althea had one major fear/:   35a

white southerners. She decided to go in spite of her fears. At the Eatons' house, Althea

had to get used to: wearing skirts, obeying rules, and getting along with people. She   35d

was expected to listen to adult conversations and join in with well-chosen comments.

At the time, Althea considered these requirements to be serious disadvantages.

However, there were also advantages to life with the Eatons, such as: regular meals, a   35d

room of her own, an allowance, and unlimited use of the doctor's private tennis court.

School presented one overwhelming social problem Althea could not make friends   35a

with either boys or girls. The boys may have resented her athletic prowess and her

self-confidence. The girls considered her a tomboy. Years later Althea still recalled

their taunts "She's no lady" and "Look at her throwing that ball just like a man." Even   35a

the singing instructor added to her woes. When he placed her in the tenor section to

make the chorus sound better, the other girls in the chorus could not control their

giggles. Some people even made fun of her tennis, but her tenacity paid off. Before

she had finished high school, Florida A&M University had offered her a scholarship.

Althea had been right to expect problems if she lived in the South, but she had not

anticipated what the problems would be. If she had put the story of those high school

years into a book, she could have titled it *The Unexpected, Problems Are Not Always*   35c

What They Seem.

Van Goor and Hacker, *Developmental Exercises for Rules for Writers*, 7th ed. (Boston: Bedford, 2012)

EXERCISE 36-1 ◆ The apostrophe: Guided practice

In the following paragraphs, add apostrophes where they are missing and delete or correct them where they are misused. The numbers in the margin refer to relevant rules in section 36 of *Rules for Writers*, Seventh Edition. The first revision has been done for you; answers to this exercise appear in the back of this book.

During the 1990 troubles in Panama, American television and newspaper

reporters had an exciting piece of news. They reported that for the first time

American female soldiers had been engaged in actual combat. Acting as her ~~soldiers~~ *soldiers'*   36a

leader, Captain Linda Bray led her troops into combat. Names of two additional

women who were involved in combat, Staff Sergeant April Hanley and Private First

Class Christina Proctor, were reported in the newspapers. Their's were the only names   36e

reported, although other women also took part in the fighting.

It wasn't the first time an American woman had fought in an American battle,

but its not likely that many people are aware of that fact. The Civil War had its   36c

female fighters too. Loreta Janeta Velazquez fought for the Confederates' in the   36e

Civil War after her husbands death. Like many other women whose husbands were   36a

killed in that war, she must have asked herself, "Whose going to take his place in   36c

battle?" The decision to fight was her's alone. Someone is sure to ask how that was   36e

possible, especially in those days. Military identification was not very sophisticated

in the 1860s. Someones willingness to fight was that person's major qualification, and   36b

each fighting unit needed to replace it's losses as fast as possible. Velazquez simply   36e

disguised herself in mens clothing, found a troop needing replacements, and joined the   36a

fight. Loreta Janeta Velazquez was Linda Brays Civil War predecessor.   36a

Van Goor and Hacker, *Developmental Exercises for Rules for Writers*, 7th ed. (Boston: Bedford, 2012)

36-1 | The apostrophe: Guided practice   **129**

EXERCISE 36-2 ◆ The apostrophe

To read about this topic, see section 36 in *Rules for Writers*, Seventh Edition.

A Each of the following sentences has two words containing apostrophes. Only one of the apostrophes is used correctly in each sentence. Delete or move the other apostrophe. Example:

Further back in American history, one woman's soldiering had made her famous; no one

hers.

has yet had a story to match ~~her's.~~
                                    ^

1. Deborah Sampson never dreamed that she would someday fight in battles' for American

    independence, much less that the battles' outcomes might depend on her.

2. Because her parents' income was not enough to support their children, her parents' sent

    Deborah to live with relatives in another town.

3. Later she was sent to live in a foster family with ten sons'; the sons' acceptance of her was

    wholehearted, and one son became her fiancé when she grew up.

4. The Revolutionary War was'nt over when news of his death reached Deborah; she wasn't

    long in making a major decision.

5. Determined that his place should become her's, she enlisted under a man's name.

B The following sentences contain no apostrophes. Add any that are needed and make any necessary corrections in spelling. If a sentence is correct, mark it "OK." Example:

Who's   who's

~~Whose~~ to say ~~whos~~ right about Deborah Sampson's decision?
  ^   ^

6. If men have the right to fight for their beliefs, should women have the right to fight for

    theirs?

7. Its clear that Deborah Sampson thought so; she enlisted twice to fight for hers.

8. On her first attempt, Sampson enlisted almost at the end of the day—and was discovered

    before its end arrived.

9. Though drinking was not a habit of hers, she spent her first evening as a soldier copying

    other new soldiers behavior.

10. Coming to the aid of this very noisy, very drunk, and very sick "buddy" of theirs, they soon

    were asking, "Whose this?"

Van Goor and Hacker, *Developmental Exercises for Rules for Writers*, 7th ed. (Boston: Bedford, 2012)

EXERCISE 36-3 ◆ The apostrophe

To read about this topic, see section 36 in *Rules for Writers*, Seventh Edition.

Circle the correct form of the words in parentheses. The first sentence has been done for you.

Loreta Velazquez was not the only woman (who's / (whose)) help was used during the Civil War, nor was being a foot soldier the only way women served in that war.

She was not in combat, but Mary Walker, then in her (thirties / thirty's), served in the Union army. She served with such distinction that she became the first woman to receive the Medal of Honor, the (military's / militarys') highest-ranking medal. It is awarded only to members of the armed (forces / force's) and only for gallantry in action.

Mary (Walker's / Walkers) specialty was surgery. Just as shocking as her profession—the role of military surgeon was not (everyone's / everyones') idea of the proper role for a woman in the 1860s—were Dr. Walker's opinions on how women should dress. She said that women (shouldn't / should'nt) wear tight corsets because such corsets were injurious to (women's / womens') health. She even considered long skirts unhealthy. She felt so strongly on the subject of women's attire that she was determined to wear long pants. Army (regulations / regulations') did not permit such attire for a woman. (Who's / Whose) permission was required for her to do so? Special permission from the US Congress was required, but Dr. Mary Walker finally won that battle of the Civil War.

She did not live to see the end of her final battle, however. After the war, she went back to her private practice of medicine and began fighting for a constitutional amendment to allow women to vote. Congress passed the Nineteenth Amendment in 1920. Unfortunately, Mary Walker died before (its / it's) adoption.

Van Goor and Hacker, *Developmental Exercises for Rules for Writers*, 7th ed. (Boston: Bedford, 2012)

36-3 | The apostrophe 131

EXERCISE 36-4 ◆ The apostrophe: Guided review

In the following paragraph, add apostrophes where they are missing and delete or correct them where they are misused. The numbers in the margin refer to relevant rules in section 36 of *Rules for Writers*, Seventh Edition. The first revision has been done for you.

Deborah Sampson, who fought in the American Revolution, fulfilled her light

infantryman duties pretending to be a private named Robert Shurtlieff. To ~~anyones~~ *anyone's*   36b

questions about where he was based, this private said, "West Point." Sampson's first

enlistment lasted less than a day, but her second enlistment was different. It lasted

until the wars end, when along with many others she was honorably discharged from   36a

the Continental army on October 23, 1783. Throughout her service, it was everyones   36b

opinion that she was an excellent soldier. Her officers reports on her were always good.   36a

Wounded twice, she outwitted the doctors' and returned to her unit undetected; but   36e

when she came down with "the fevers," a doctor discovered the secret that until then

had been her's alone. (Many of the distinctions among different illnesses that produce   36e

fevers—from typhoid to influenza—were not yet known; if patients had a high fever

and it's accompanying discomforts for very long, they were diagnosed as having   36e

"the fevers.") Its no surprise that when her secret was finally revealed, her superior   36c

officers couldnt believe it. Dressed in women's clothes, she was escorted to separate   36c

quarters not by the military police but by her superior officers. Many years later, at

Paul Reveres' suggestion, she donned the uniform again and went on speaking tours'   36a, 36e

to raise much-needed money for her family and to secure a monthly pension from the

army she had once served.

Van Goor and Hacker, *Developmental Exercises for Rules for Writers*, 7th ed. (Boston: Bedford, 2012)

EXERCISE 37-1 ♦ Quotation marks: Guided practice

Edit the following sentences to correct the use of quotation marks and of punctuation with quotation marks. The numbers in the margin refer to relevant rules in section 37 of *Rules for Writers*, Seventh Edition. Answers to this exercise appear in the back of this book. Example:

> **The parents watched as the doctor bandaged the boy's eyes. "For the love of**   37e
>
> **God, what can we do ? " asked the father .**

1. The doctor answered "You can do nothing but pray."   37e

2. When the bandages were removed and the shades were opened to let in the   37e
   bright sunlight, the doctor asked, "What do you see"?

3. "Nothing," said the boy. I see nothing.   37a

4. The village priest said "I have recently seen a remarkable school." He had just   37e
   returned from a trip to Paris.

5. "In this school, he added blind students are taught to read."   37a

6. "You didn't say "read," did you?" asked the boy's father.   37b

7. The boy responded to the priest's words as if they were a trick of some kind   37e
   "Now you are joking with me. How can such a thing be possible?"

8. The boy, Louis, thought it would be "great fun" to visit that school someday.   37f

9. His father promised "We will go soon, Louis."   37c

10. And so it happened that ten-year-old Louis Braille entered the National   37d
    Institute for Blind Youths and began the long effort to erase the fear people had
    of even the word blind.

Van Goor and Hacker, *Developmental Exercises for Rules for Writers*, 7th ed. (Boston: Bedford, 2012)

37-1 | Quotation marks: Guided practice   **133**

EXERCISE 37-2 ◆ Quotation marks

To read about this topic, see section 37 in *Rules for Writers*, Seventh Edition.

Change each indirect quotation into a direct quotation, using correct punctuation and deleting or changing words as necessary. Example:

> **The doctor told them not to look for miracles.**
>
> *The doctor said, "Do not look for miracles."* _____
>
> _____

1. The doctor added that in all probability their son would never see again.

   _____

   _____

2. Mr. Braille exclaimed that he had seen blind students at the institute making their own

   clothes and shoes.

   _____

   _____

3. The inventor of the raised-dot system of writing used in the military told Louis to

   experiment all he wished but not to set his hopes too high.

   _____

   _____

4. When his old friends in the village saw him with his stylus and paper, they asked him if he

   was still punching away at it.

   _____

   _____

5. Louis asked the government official if he was blind and if he understood what it was like not

   to see.

   _____

   _____

Van Goor and Hacker, *Developmental Exercises for Rules for Writers*, 7th ed. (Boston: Bedford, 2012)

EXERCISE 37-3 ◆ Quotation marks

To read about this topic, see section 37 in *Rules for Writers*, Seventh Edition.

In the following sentences, insert needed quotation marks and punctuation used with quotation marks. If a sentence is correct, mark it "OK." Example:

> **One of Braille's students wrote, "Attending his classes was a pleasure to enjoy rather than a duty to fulfill."**

1. Louis Braille asked the inventor of the raised-dot system of writing a serious question "Do you think it would be possible to change the symbols in some way, to reduce them in size?"

2. Barbier, the inventor of the system, replied "Of course. Anything is possible."

3. "I have hoped" said the founder of the institute "that this school would be a bright torch held aloft to bring light to the blind."

4. "I am going to instruct the teachers to begin using your system in the classroom," said the institute director. "You must understand, though, that your method has not yet been proved."

5. Louis Braille wanted a system so complete that blind people could read and write the words and music to a song like the Marseillaise, the French national anthem.

Van Goor and Hacker, *Developmental Exercises for
Rules for Writers*, 7th ed. (Boston: Bedford, 2012)

37-3 | Quotation marks **135**

EXERCISE 37-4 ◆ Quotation marks: Guided review

Edit the following paragraphs to correct the use of quotation marks and of punctuation used with quotation marks. The numbers in the margin refer to relevant rules in section 37 of *Rules for Writers*, Seventh Edition. The first correction has been made for you.

Louis Braille entered the National Institute for Blind Youths in Paris when he

was ten. At twelve, he was already experimenting with a system of raised dots on

paper known as "night-~~writing~~", *writing,"* which was used by the military. Institute teachers   37e

decided that night-writing was impractical, but Louis became proficient at it. When

Charles Barbier, inventor of the system, visited the institute, Louis told him "Your   37e

symbols are too large and too complicated. Impressed, Barbier encouraged him and   37a

said that "since Louis was blind himself, he might discover the magic key that had   37f

eluded his teachers."

Louis Braille wanted a system that could transcribe everything from a textbook

on science to a poem like Heinrich Heine's Loreley. At fifteen, he had worked out his   37c

own system of six dots arranged in various patterns. "Read to me," he said to one of his

teachers, and I will take down your words." As the teacher read, Louis punched dots   37e

onto his paper and then read the passage back without error. The teacher exclaimed,

"Remarkable"! Government officials, not impressed enough to take any action, said   37e

simply that Braille should be encouraged. "You didn't say "encouraged," did you?"   37b

asked Braille. He wanted official acceptance, not simply encouragement. "The system

has proved itself," said Louis. We have been using it for five years now."   37e

For most people, the word Braille itself now means simply a system of   37d

reading and writing used by blind people; for blind people, it means freedom and

independence. Braille himself died before his system was recognized beyond the

institute. The plaque on the house of his birth, however, records the world's recognition

of his work with these words: He opened the doors of knowledge to all those who   37a

cannot see.

Van Goor and Hacker, *Developmental Exercises for Rules for Writers*, 7th ed. (Boston: Bedford, 2012)

EXERCISE 38-1 ◆ End punctuation: Guided practice

Supply end punctuation—period, question mark, or exclamation point—as needed in the following paragraphs. The numbers in the margin refer to relevant rules in section 38 of *Rules for Writers*, Seventh Edition. The first and last revisions have been done for you; answers to this exercise appear in the back of this book.

After Louis Braille invented his new system that would allow blind people to

read and write, he tested it thoroughly. Students and faculty of the National Institute   38a

for Blind Youths were excited at how easily they could master it. They encouraged

Louis to demonstrate the system to the French educational authorities, who made the

rules for the institute Louis agreed to do so   38a, 38a

When Louis held the demonstration, all went well What excitement he and his   38a

friends felt But the authorities would not recommend that the institute adopt Louis's   38c

new system Why didn't the French authorities recognize the advantages of Braille's   38a

system Did they have a vested interest in the old system of teaching the blind Or a   38b, 38b

real doubt about the new system Whatever their reasons, they delayed the pleasures   38b

of reading for thousands of people In addition, a new director, Dr. Pignier, even   38a

outlawed the use of the system at the institute for four years   38a

Although unhappy and disheartened, Braille never gave up; he knew his system

would enable the blind to read.   38a

EXERCISE 38-2 ♦ End punctuation

To read about this topic, see section 38 in *Rules for Writers*, Seventh Edition.

Supply end punctuation—period, question mark, or exclamation point—for each of the following sentences. At least one sentence of each pair is a question. Example:

   a.   Louis asked if he could demonstrate his technique at the institute.

   b.   Louis asked, "May I demonstrate my technique at the ~~institute"~~ *institute?"*

1. a.   What Louis had figured out was a new code

    b.   What had Louis figured out

2. a.   What should he do about teaching it

    b.   What to do about teaching it was the next decision to make

3. a.   Who could help him test the system was another question

    b.   Who could help him test the system

4. a.   How extraordinary it was that a leatherworker's son should have such talent

    b.   How was it that he had such extraordinary talent

5. a.   Why did he never give up, either as a child or as an adult

    b.   Why he never gave up, either as a child or as an adult, puzzled many of his friends

Van Goor and Hacker, *Developmental Exercises for Rules for Writers*, 7th ed. (Boston: Bedford, 2012)

EXERCISE 38-3 ◆ End punctuation: Guided review

Supply appropriate end punctuation—period, question mark, or exclamation point—in the following paragraphs. The numbers in the margin refer to relevant rules in section 38 of *Rules for Writers*, Seventh Edition. The first revision has been done for you.

Braille's reading and writing system depended on a group of six dots. He called this group a "cell." He conceived of the cell as three rows with space for two dots on each row. But he did not have to put two dots on each row, and he did not have to use all three rows. Figuring it this way, Braille counted sixty-three possible arrangements   38a for the dots. Using these possibilities, Braille worked out an alphabet. Then he added punctuation marks and numerals. But he still was not satisfied. There was something else that he wanted to do.

Braille knew very well that blindness does not keep someone from becoming proficient at a particular skill. Like many other blind people, Braille himself was an accomplished musician. As a young boy at the National Institute for Blind Youths, he had learned to play several instruments. But he could play only by ear Louis Braille   38a wanted to be able to read music, play what he read, and then write music that other musicians could read and play.

When Braille was only fifteen, he devised a way to write music using his six-dot cell. As soon as he knew it was workable, he wanted a piano of his own to try it on. By saving his small salary, he was able to buy a piano. Next he wanted lessons Paris had   38a many good music teachers. Braille took lessons from some of the best and then began to teach piano and violoncello at the institute. He also gave frequent piano recitals throughout Paris.

When he knew he was good on the piano, Braille said it was time to play something else "God's music," the church organ, was what he wanted to learn. With   38a great effort he learned to manage the foot pedals, the double keyboard, and the rows of stops St. Nicholas-des-Champs Church hired him as its organist. However, Braille   38a found himself so busy thinking about stops and pedals that he couldn't keep up with the service at first. Did he resign Of course not Braille simply became so familiar with   38b, 38c the music that he did not have to think about it and could follow the church service as it went along Louis Braille may have been the first blind organist in Paris, but he was not the last. In Braille's lifetime, the institute's music director placed more than fifty blind organists in the city. 38a

Many people have wondered where Braille got the idea of adapting his new system to music. Did it come from one of his teachers Or one of his friends Or from his own mind? However it happened, he adapted the Braille system for music, and again Braille opened a new world to the blind. What an extraordinary gift this was Except for sight itself, could anyone have given blind musicians a greater gift 38b, 38b 38c 38b

Van Goor and Hacker, *Developmental Exercises for Rules for Writers*, 7th ed. (Boston: Bedford, 2012)

Note: For exercises 39-1 to 39-4 and the review exercise on page 146, you will need to refer to the following poem.

The New Colossus

by Emma Lazarus

Not like the brazen giant of Greek fame,

With conquering limbs astride from land to land;

Here at our sea-washed, sunset gates shall stand

A mighty woman with a torch, whose flame

Is the imprisoned lightning, and her name

Mother of Exiles. From her beacon hand

Glows world-wide welcome; her mild eyes command

The air-bridged harbor that twin cities frame.

"Keep, ancient lands, your storied pomp!" cries she

With silent lips. "Give me your tired, your poor,

Your huddled masses yearning to breathe free,

The wretched refuse of your teeming shore,

Send these, the homeless, tempest-tost to me,

I lift my lamp beside the golden door."

Van Goor and Hacker, *Developmental Exercises for Rules for Writers,* 7th ed. (Boston: Bedford, 2012)

39 | Other punctuation marks   **141**

EXERCISE 39-1 ◆ Other punctuation marks: Guided practice

Edit the following paragraphs for correct use of the dash, parentheses, brackets, the ellipsis mark, and the slash. Refer to the poem "The New Colossus" (p. 141) as necessary. The numbers in the margin refer to relevant rules in section 39 of *Rules for Writers*, Seventh Edition. The first revision has been done for you; answers to this exercise appear in the back of this book.

The most famous woman in America is Miss Liberty͵ a 450,000-pound, 154-foot   39a

resident of New York City. For people all over the world, the Statue of Liberty

symbolizes America. Yet the idea for the statue came not from America, England, or

even New York itself, but from France. Three men can claim credit for the construction   39a

of Miss Liberty: 1. Frédéric-Auguste Bartholdi, sculptor; 2. Alexandre-Gustave Eiffel,   39b

structural engineer; and 3. Richard Morris Hunt, architect. France gave the statue to

the United States, and the United States provided the pedestal—on which it stands.   39a

Two Americans contributed significantly to the statue. The first was Joseph

Pulitzer, then owner and publisher of the *New York World* (and a Russian immigrant).   39b

He led several fundraising efforts and urged every American to give what he/she could   39e

to help build the pedestal. The second American who contributed significantly was

Emma Lazarus. She wrote the famous lines on the bronze plaque inside the statue.

Her three-word title "The New Colossus" (which means "huge statue") alludes to a

statue built in the harbor of Rhodes in ancient Greece. The most quoted lines from

"The New Colossus" are probably these: "Give me your tired, your poor, / Your huddled

masses yearning to breathe free."

Van Goor and Hacker, *Developmental Exercises for Rules for Writers*, 7th ed. (Boston: Bedford, 2012)

EXERCISE 39-2 ◆ Other punctuation marks

To read about this topic, see section 39 in *Rules for Writers*, Seventh Edition.

Edit the following sentences by using the punctuation indicated in brackets. Refer to the poem "The New Colossus" (p. 141) as necessary. Example:

> Bartholdi's Statue of Liberty better known in France as Liberty Enlightening the World celebrated ideals that France and America shared. [Dashes]

1. The American Revolution celebrated liberty. The French added two more words to form the battle cry of the French Revolution, "Liberty, Equality, and Fraternity." [Dash]

2. Emma Lazarus understood Bartholdi's desire to demonstrate this shared ideal. In her opening line, "Not like the brazen giant of Greek fame" (the Colossus of Rhodes), she alludes to an ancient statue one hundred feet high. [Brackets]

3. Bartholdi was determined to build "A mighty woman—Mother of Exiles" and place her in New York Harbor. [Ellipsis mark]

4. He traveled all over America, to Boston, Chicago, Denver, Salt Lake City, and many other places, to promote his idea. [Dashes]

5. He was amazed at the country's size, industry, and enthusiasm for creating things, buildings, that is, not art. [Parentheses]

6. Bartholdi discovered that money, the enthusiasm of US citizens, and political support, all necessary for his project, were hard to get. [Parentheses]

7. He decided on a novel, hands-on approach, allowing people to climb into completed parts of the statue. [Dash]

8. Three cities were chosen: [1] In Philadelphia, the statue's hand and torch attracted Centennial Exhibition visitors; [2] in New York, the same exhibit drew people downtown; and [3] in Paris, visitors explored the statue's head and shoulders. [Parentheses]

9. When more money was needed, wealthy newspaper publisher Joseph Pulitzer, an immigrant himself, turned to nonwealthy Americans, working-class men, women, and children, and it was their small gifts that paid for the statue's pedestal. [Dashes]

10. Their gifts allowed Miss Liberty's torch to shine out over the water to say, "Send these, the homeless, tempest-tost to me, I lift my lamp beside the golden door." [Slash]

EXERCISE 39-3 ◆ Other punctuation marks

To read about this topic, see section 39 in *Rules for Writers*, Seventh Edition.

The dashes, parentheses, brackets, ellipsis marks, and slashes in the following sentences are not well used. Edit the sentences to be more effective by deleting punctuation marks, replacing them with other marks, or restructuring the sentences. Refer to "The New Colossus" (p. 141) as necessary. Example:

> On October 29, 1886 ,∕ one hundred and ten years after the signing of the Declaration of
>
> Independence ,∕ Miss Liberty was formally dedicated.

1. Miss Liberty was the only woman at her dedication (except for two Frenchwomen who came with the sculptor).

2. On that day, the Lady whose "beacon hand/Glow(ed) world-wide welcome" was almost obscured from view by rain and wind.

3. Also, the crowds of people pushing and shoving resembled the ". . . huddled masses" Emma Lazarus wrote about.

4. The crowd—crushed together—trying to listen to the main speaker—he was William M. Evarts—could hear other voices too.

5. Women who were angry about being excluded from the ceremony had sailed in close to the island (they had chartered a boat) and were yelling their protests.

6. With all of the noise from the crowd and/or the women, the speaker paused.

7. He paused so long that an aide thought the speech was over. The aide signaled Bartholdi (who was waiting inside the statue).

8. Bartholdi saw the signal and unveiled the statue . . . an hour early.

9. The plaque with Emma Lazarus's poem on it was not on the statue at this time; it was added later—in 1903—without any special ceremony.

10. It is still there today for all visitors to read/ponder as they meet America's most beloved lady.

Van Goor and Hacker, *Developmental Exercises for Rules for Writers*, 7th ed. (Boston: Bedford, 2012)

EXERCISE 39-4 ◆ Other punctuation marks: Guided review

Edit the following paragraphs for the most effective use of the dash, parentheses, brackets, the ellipsis mark, and the slash. Refer to "The New Colossus" (p. 141) as necessary. The numbers in the margin refer to relevant rules in section 39 of *Rules for Writers*, Seventh Edition. The first revision has been done for you.

fourteen-line

The sonnet is a poem ~~/ of fourteen lines /~~ with a particular pattern to its   39a

rhymes; it is often used to compare or contrast two items. Emma Lazarus's poem "The

New Colossus" is a sonnet. Lazarus uses its fourteen lines to contrast two statues.

The ancient Colossus of Rhodes (which was male) represented the sun god; the new   39b

Colossus was female and represented liberty. The Rhodes Colossus symbolized what

Lazarus calls "storied pomp." The French-made American statue stood for freedom and

opportunity.

In her first line, "Not like the brazen (bronze) giant of Greek fame," Lazarus   39c

refers to the material of which the old Colossus was made. Bronze, a valuable metal

when the Colossus of Rhodes was erected in 280 BC, was available only to the wealthy.

Miss Liberty was made of copper, a material available to all classes of people. When

Miss Liberty was erected in 1898, America's least valuable coin—the one-cent piece,   39a

was made from copper. Miss Liberty was for everyone, not just the wealthy.

The major contrast Lazarus sets up is in the attitudes of the two statues. The

old Colossus is powerful, not caring about the ". . . wretched refuse" of its "teeming   39d

shore." The new one welcomes all: "Send these, the homeless, tempest-tost to me, I lift   39e

my lamp beside the golden door."

Van Goor and Hacker, *Developmental Exercises for Rules for Writers*, 7th ed. (Boston: Bedford, 2012)

39-4 | Other punctuation marks: Guided review   **145**

REVIEW OF 32–39 ◆ Punctuation

Edit the following paragraphs to correct errors in punctuation or to use more effective punctuation. Refer to the poem "The New Colossus" (p. 141) as necessary. The numbers in the margin refer to relevant rules in sections 32–39 of *Rules for Writers*, Seventh Edition. The first revision has been done for you.

The outside of the Statue of Liberty is made of copper, but what is inside the   32a

statue. Inside the statue are: iron braces and staircases. The thin copper plates that   38b, 35d

form the outside of the statue are bolted to a network of iron braces. There are several

staircases allowing workers and tourists to climb all the way into the head and the

torch. (This intricate network of braces and stairways was designed by Alexandre-

Gustave Eiffel; the same man who designed the famous Eiffel Tower in Paris.)   34d

For some years, the lighting equipment for Miss Libertys torch was also inside.   36a

Soon after the statue was set up for example engineers tried Edison's new invention,   32f

the electric lightbulb. They cut holes in the torch's copper sheets and hung lightbulbs

inside. Later, the copper sheets came down and glass windows went up. Giving Miss

Liberty a light that everyone would recognize as hers, challenged engineers and   33b

designers for sixty more years. When the statue was restored in the 1980s part of   32b

the lighting equipment was moved outside. Floodlights were installed on the torch's

balcony, and focused on thin gold sheets that form the torch "... whose flame / Is the   33a, 39d

imprisoned lightning. Miss Liberty will be able to welcome newcomers for many years.   37a

Van Goor and Hacker, *Developmental Exercises for Rules for Writers*, 7th ed. (Boston: Bedford, 2012)

EXERCISE 40/41/42-1 ◆ Abbreviations, numbers, and italics: Guided practice

Correct any errors in abbreviations, numbers, and italics in the following paragraphs. The numbers in the margin refer to relevant rules in sections 40, 41, and 42 of *Rules for Writers*, Seventh Edition. The first revision has been done for you; a suggested revision of these paragraphs appears in the back of this book.

Everyone has heard of Christopher Columbus, but not many people know much
                                                            AD 1492.
about him. Most people learn that he discovered America in ~~1492 AD.~~ Some people   40c
know that he had three ships, and they might be able to name them. (The ships were
the "Niña," the "Pinta," and the "Santa María.") A few people might even remember   42b
that Columbus thought he had found the Indies. And those with great self-confidence
might be willing to guess at the number of trips he made to his Indies. (It was 4.)   41a
Probably no one could tell you his favorite word, adelante.   42d

If they were asked what Columbus was trying to prove with his expensive
journey, most people would reply that he was trying to prove that the world is round.
They would be wrong. If they were asked what Columbus meant by the term Indies,   42d
they would probably say "India." They would be wrong again. If they were asked what
Columbus's rank was, they would most likely say "captain." They would be wrong
again. If they were asked what his sailors feared most, a no. of them would reply,   40e
"They feared that the boats would fall off the edge of the earth." And they would be
wrong again.

Isn't it strange that people can be so ignorant about a well-known man like
Columbus?

EXERCISE 40/41/42-2 ◆ Abbreviations and numbers

To read about this topic, see sections 40 and 41 in *Rules for Writers*, Seventh Edition.

 A Edit the following sentences to correct errors in the use of abbreviations. Mark the one correct sentence "OK." Example:

The sailors who voyaged with Columbus used the same four directions sailors still use:
north, south, east, and west.
~~N, S, E, and W.~~
^

1. Sailors in AD 1492 knew the world was round; they were not afraid of sailing off the edge of the world.

2. They worried about more serious things—e.g., whether the wind would blow both ways so they could get back to Spain.

3. They also weren't sure about distances; however, one famous Italian prof., Dr. Toscanelli, thought he knew.

4. He was willing to estimate the distance from Lisbon, Port., to Japan.

5. He said that the exact no. of miles between the two places was three thousand nautical miles.

B Edit the following sentences to correct errors in the use of numbers. Mark the one correct sentence "OK." Example:

three
Dr. Toscanelli set the distance at 3 thousand nautical miles.
^

6. In twelve ninety-eight, Marco Polo wrote a book about his travels to the Indies.

7. 7,448 islands were in the Indies, according to Marco Polo's book.

8. Columbus was 41 when he convinced Queen Isabella to send him to find those islands.

9. As part of the contract, Columbus demanded ten % of the treasure he brought back to Spain.

10. At 8:00 a.m. on August 3, 1492, Columbus set out from Spain for the Indies.

Van Goor and Hacker, *Developmental Exercises for Rules for Writers*, 7th ed. (Boston: Bedford, 2012)

EXERCISE 40/41/42-3 ◆ Italics (underlining)

To read about this topic, see section 42 in *Rules for Writers*, Seventh Edition.

Edit the following sentences to correct the use of italics. Example:

> *Description of the World.*
> **Marco Polo's book was titled ~~"Description of the World."~~**
>   ^

1. On the "Niña," the "Pinta," and the "Santa María," Columbus brought along one hundred men, all kinds of supplies, and enough cats to control the rat population.

2. Columbus always spoke the same word to his men—Adelante! (That means "Forward!" or "Sail on!")

3. Marco Polo's book had not prepared the men for seeing the same horizon week after week, seemingly ad infinitum.

4. To every fear or complaint, Columbus simply replied "Forward!" and that word forward began to get on the sailors' nerves.

5. Finally, Columbus's fleet made landfall on several groups of islands, some of which Columbus named after stories he had read in the *Bible* about King Solomon's travels and treasures.

Van Goor and Hacker, *Developmental Exercises for Rules for Writers*, 7th ed. (Boston: Bedford, 2012)

40/41/42-3 | Italics (underlining)   **149**

EXERCISE 40/41/42-4 ◆ Abbreviations, numbers, and italics: Guided review

Correct any errors in the use of abbreviations, numbers, and italics in the following paragraphs. The numbers in the margin refer to relevant rules in sections 40, 41, and 42 of *Rules for Writers*, Seventh Edition. The first revision has been done for you.

                                         AD

Columbus's first voyage, in 1492, ~~AD~~, was successful. Pleased with the gifts he   40c

had brought back and impressed by his reports, King Ferdinand and Queen Isabella

quickly ordered him to organize another voyage. Columbus was delighted to do so. At

first his luck held. Led by the flagship Maríagalante, a fleet of 17 ships and a thousand   42b, 41a

men who wanted to colonize the new land made the second trip in twenty-one days.

Columbus's good fortune, however, did not last. Life went downhill for the Italian

sailor from that time on.

    The so-called Admiral of the Ocean Seas (a title Columbus had given himself)

had one disastrous experience after another. When he got back to the recently settled

town he had left, the whole settlement had been destroyed, and the 39 men he had left   41a

there were all dead. Columbus quickly found a new spot for his new colony, the first

European colony in America. The new site had serious drawbacks, e.g., bad water and   40d

many mosquitoes. Embarrassed, Columbus had to send Queen Isabella's ships back

for help; he loaded them not with gold but with pepper, sandalwood, and a no. of   40e

exotic birds.

    Other voyages followed, but each turned out worse than the one before it. Not

even his favorite word, *adelante*, seemed to work for Columbus anymore. His first

voyage had definitely been the most successful.

Van Goor and Hacker, *Developmental Exercises for Rules for Writers*, 7th ed. (Boston: Bedford, 2012)

EXERCISE 43/44/45-1 ◆ Spelling, the hyphen, and capitalization: Guided practice

Edit the following paragraphs to correct misspellings and errors in the use of the hyphen and capitalization. The numbers in the margin refer to relevant rules in sections 43, 44, and 45 of *Rules for Writers*, Seventh Edition. The first revision has been done for you; a revision of these paragraphs appears in the back of this book.

Columbus's return to Spain from his first exploration was difficult. The *Niña* and the *Pinta* were separated, the *Niña* almost sank, and the governor on the island of Santa María had put Columbus's whole crew in jail. It seemed a miracle that both boats survived there journeys and arrived in the harbor at Palos on the same day.　43c

As difficult as that return was, the reception at court quite made up for it. Columbus certainly made an all out effort to impress the court, the city, and the entire　44d country. Lavishly attired, he recieved a grand welcome as he led his entourage into　43a Barcelona, the spanish capital. It must have been a sight to behold: A procession like　45a, 45f none Barcelona had ever seen before. Leading the parade was a gaudily-bedecked　44b horse carrying Columbus, followed by six captive "indians" and all the crew. Everyone　45a but Columbus was carrying boxes, baskets, and cages full of interesting and exotic items.

When the group reached the throne room, King Ferdinand and Queen Isabella stood up to greet Columbus formally and to admire his apron covered captives.　44b Columbus asked the royal couple to except gifts of plants, shells, darts, thread, and　43c gold. As intrigued as they were with the other gifts, King Ferdinand and Queen Isabella basically wanted the gold. Luckily, Columbus had collected enough of it to satisfy them.

By the end of his first week home, Columbus had such prestige that everyone wanted to accomodate the wishes of the Italian sailor at the court of Spain. Columbus　43d had no doubt that he would receive a Commission for a second voyage of exploration　45a or even colonization.

EXERCISE 43/44/45-2 ◆ Spelling

To read about this topic, see section 43 in *Rules for Writers*, Seventh Edition.

Edit the following sentences to correct spelling errors. (Hint: There are ten errors.) Example:

>   *incredibly*   *believed*
> **Others may have considered him ~~incredibally~~ lucky, but Columbus ~~beleived~~ he had been called by God to be the one to find a new sea route to the Indies.**

1. To begin with, he was born in Genoa, Italy, the best place concievable for someone who wanted to be in the sailing busness, since Genoa was a major seaport.

2. Other people said his being born there was all "just chance"; Columbus prefered to think that it was part of God's arrangment for him.

3. He was not suprised to be the sole survivor of a shipwreck that occured when he was twenty-five.

4. Weather others excepted the idea or not, Columbus knew he survived such a disasterous event because God had plans for him.

5. He thought that even his name emphasized his calling: *Christopher* means "Christ-bearing," and he would take Christ's name to the "heatherns" in India.

Van Goor and Hacker, *Developmental Exercises for Rules for Writers,* 7th ed. (Boston: Bedford, 2012)

EXERCISE 43/44/45-3 ◆ The hyphen

To read about this topic, see section 44 in *Rules for Writers*, Seventh Edition.

The writer of the following sentences got hyphen-happy. Remove six of the eleven hyphens. If a sentence needs no hyphens removed, mark it "OK." Example:

> **Columbus's all-consuming goal made him think that God~~-~~himself had worked~~-~~out the fortuitous marriage Columbus made in 1478.**

1. Marrying into a noble-family when he was thirty-three gave Columbus direct-access to the king of Portugal.

2. When the king firmly-declined Columbus's request to finance an exploratory-voyage, this well-known sailor decided he was supposed to go to Spain.

3. Queen Isabella was determined to make everyone into a practicing-Christian; because Columbus was religious, she did not consider the voyage a half-witted proposal.

4. After his discovery of "India," Columbus received confirmation of his self-given title, Admiral of the Ocean Seas and Viceroy of the Indies.

5. When the *Santa María* was wrecked, Columbus saw the incident as his God-given opportunity to go back posthaste to Spain, recruit more men, and return to this newly-found land.

Van Goor and Hacker, *Developmental Exercises for Rules for Writers*, 7th ed. (Boston: Bedford, 2012)

43/44/45-3 | The hyphen   **153**

EXERCISE 43/44/45-4 ♦ Capitalization

To read about this topic, see section 45 in *Rules for Writers*, Seventh Edition.

Edit the following paragraphs to correct errors in capitalization. The first sentence has been edited for you. You should find ten more errors.

If Columbus had made his return trip first, he might not have been so eager to set out for
Indies.
the ~~indies.~~ The voyage turned out all right, but it had its bad times.
  ^

To begin with, the *Niña* and the *Pinta* were separated on the way back to Spain. The weather was very bad, especially when the two ships ran into a storm west of the Azores. The *Niña* almost sank. Columbus was so sure it was going down that he put a record of his Discoveries in a small barrel, sealed it completely, and threw it overboard. That way, if the ship went down, there was still a chance that someone would learn of his discoveries. Actually, the ship made it to Santa María, a portuguese island. The governor there thought Columbus was lying about his adventures and arrested the crew. The crew was released only because Columbus threatened to shoot up the town.

The *Niña* was thrown off course again, but then Columbus's luck turned. The boat came into Lisbon, and Columbus was a guest of king John II for a brief time before he took off for Spain again. finally, the *Niña* made it home. On March 15, 1493, it sailed into the harbor at Palos. The *Pinta* arrived shortly afterward on the same day. Such a coincidence certainly seemed to be a sign of Divine approval and delighted Columbus. When queen Isabella saw what Columbus had brought back, she was impressed. She thought that god had surely had a hand in the matter. Certainly many influences had played a part in his success that Spring. Even Marco Polo's book *Description of the world* had played a role: Getting Columbus started on the journey. Columbus was convinced that his life was just one miracle after another. "I've been chosen," he might have said. "God has chosen me."

Van Goor and Hacker, *Developmental Exercises for Rules for Writers*, 7th ed. (Boston: Bedford, 2012)

EXERCISE 43/44/45-5 ◆ Spelling, the hyphen, and capitalization: Guided review

Correct any errors in spelling or in the use of the hyphen or capitalization in the following paragraphs. The numbers in the margin refer to relevant rules in sections 43, 44, and 45 of *Rules for Writers*, Seventh Edition. The first revision has been done for you.

After being feted, feasted, and honored on his return from his first voyage across

                                         retold

the ocean, Columbus must have told and ~~re-told~~ the story of his trip. He would have   44a

told listeners how, after the ships had sailed for twenty one days, his men threatened   44c

to turn back because they had never sailed so far west before. Columbus, sure of

his special calling as an explorer, promised them that they would sight land within

three days. On the evening of the third day, at ten o'clock, he thought he saw a light

and alerted a nearby servant. Both of them lost sight of it almost at once. But at two

o'clock the next morning, a cannon shot sounded from the *Pinta*. "Land! Land!" cried

the sailors. Columbus had kept his promise. No wonder he began to sign his name

with a secret code to show that he was more special then other people.   43c

Retelling the story of his voyage, Columbus would have described the beautiful

Island that the ships first landed on. He named it San Salvador. He would have told   45a

how, at every island he and his men visited, natives had flocked to the boats to see the

strangers. One day, more than a thousand people had come in just one hour. Columbus

had spent three months exploring and setting up a fort before leaving for the return

trip to Spain. And on their return, eight months later, he and his crew had recieved a   43a

royal welcome.

Yes, he had had a few problems on the trip out, and the return trip had been

very hard, but one set of memories was indelibly imprinted on Columbus's brain: The   45f

memories of that remarkably successful first voyage.

REVIEW OF 40–45 ◆ Mechanics

This essay has eleven errors in spelling and mechanics. The numbers in the margin refer to relevant rules in sections 40–45 of *Rules for Writers*, Seventh Edition. The first correction has been made for you. Find and correct ten more errors.

Columbus made an all-out effort to find the Indies—India, China, the East   44d

Indies, and Japan. Instead, he found Cuba, Venezuela, the Bahamas, and the Coasts   45a

of South and Central America. Unable to find gold, he captured 500 natives and had   41a

them shipped back to Spain to be sold as slaves. He punished the natives so severely

when they did not bring him gold that in two years one third of them ran away or   44c

were killed or sold. Things went from bad to worse; e.g., many settlers died of illness,   40d

and some went back to Spain with bad reports of Columbus's governance. Convinced

that God was unhappy with him for some transgression, Columbus returned to Spain

wearing a monk's course garb and walking humbly. People gave him a new title: 43c

Columbus, Admiral of the Mosquitoes.

Ferdinand and Isabella gave him another opportunity, though, and on May

thirtieth, 1498, Columbus set out again. The voyage was disasterous, with Columbus   41b, 43d

ending up back in Spain, this time in chains. Columbus got one more chance, but

hurricanes and storms plagued him. He wrote, "other tempests have I seen, but none   45e

so long or so grim as this." He must by now have realized that Dr. Toscanelli did not no   43c

his geography very well. Yet "Sail on!" was still his answer to every setback.

When Columbus got back to Spain, sick and exhausted, queen Isabella died   45b

before he could see her. Columbus himself died still insisting he had found the Indies.

He had not, of course. He had done far more: He had discovered a "new world."

Van Goor and Hacker, *Developmental Exercises for Rules for Writers*, 7th ed. (Boston: Bedford, 2012)

EXERCISE 46-1 ◆ Parts of speech: Preview

To read about this topic, see section 46 in *Rules for Writers*, Seventh Edition.

In the following paragraphs, label the part of speech of each italicized word. Use these codes: noun (N), pronoun (PN), helping verb (HV), main verb (MV), adjective (ADJ), adverb (ADV), preposition (P), conjunction (C). The first word has been labeled for you; answers to this exercise appear in the back of this book.

                                                             MV
    America's Declaration of Independence *seems* very formal to today's *readers*. Many of its

sentences *are* long and involved, and some *of* its words seem old-fashioned. But *its* central message

is loud *and* clear to all those who take the time to read and understand it, whether they are

schoolchildren *or* adult immigrants.

    Those somewhat *formal* words contain both a declaration and a promise. The Declaration

starts with a seventy-one-word statement called the "Preamble." It *simply* says that when one

group of people break their ties *with* another, those people *should* tell *everyone* their reasons for

breaking up.

    In the next part, called the "Declaration of Rights," the colonists list their basic assumptions

about life—that everyone is born with *certain* rights ("life, liberty, and the pursuit of happiness");

that governments have power only *when* people give it to *them*; and that when a government

repeatedly *acts* in ways that deny people's rights, people have a right and a duty to overthrow that

government and build another one.

    It was a *bold* beginning for a bold document—a declaration promising freedom that has

been celebrated by Americans for more than two hundred years.

Van Goor and Hacker, *Developmental Exercises for Rules for Writers*, 7th ed. (Boston: Bedford, 2012)

46-1 | Parts of speech: Preview   **157**

EXERCISE 46-2 ◆ Nouns and noun/adjectives

To read about this topic, see section 46a in *Rules for Writers*, Seventh Edition.

A Each of the following groups of three words contains only one noun. Circle the noun. Example:

national	**nationwide**	(**nation**)

1.	defendable	defend	defenses
2.	speaking	speaker	speak
3.	just	justice	justly
4.	normal	normally	normality
5.	repetition	repeating	repeated

B Underline each noun (including noun/adjectives) in the following sentences. Examples:

When they apply for American <u>citizenship</u>, <u>refugee</u> <u>immigrants</u> must study some famous American <u>documents</u>.

6. Schoolchildren and new citizens have similar homework assignments.

7. They both must learn the Pledge of Allegiance to the country's flag.

8. Many of these people also memorize the opening words of the Declaration of Independence.

9. The Preamble to the Constitution is often assigned, as well as some famous speeches and the national anthem.

10. If students pass their tests on all of this, they are promoted; if immigrants pass theirs, they are welcomed into American citizenship.

Van Goor and Hacker, *Developmental Exercises for Rules for Writers*, 7th ed. (Boston: Bedford, 2012)

EXERCISE 46-3 ◆ Nouns and noun/adjectives

To read about this topic, see section 46a in *Rules for Writers*, Seventh Edition.

All of the following paired sentences contain some form of the word *exhibit*. In each pair, circle the letter of the sentence that uses the word *exhibit* as a noun or noun/adjective; be prepared to explain how you know it is a noun. (Hint: There is only one noun/adjective.) Example:

(**a.**) The Declaration of Independence is on exhibit at the National Archives in Washington, DC.

b. The Archives exhibits the Declaration of Independence for many tourist groups.

1. a. Many people do not realize that the exhibits in the national museums change frequently.

   b. Each museum exhibits a wide variety of materials.

2. a. Museums can exhibit something of interest to almost any visitor.

   b. It is impossible to predict which exhibit any one visitor will enjoy.

3. a. Most children prefer an interactive exhibit over any other kind.

   b. The children can exhibit their own skill in operating the interactive devices.

4. a. Most of the exhibit halls have excellent signs and explanations about what the visitor can see.

   b. Curators can exhibit rare items safely in specially constructed cases.

5. a. When the museums are exhibiting items borrowed from another place, visitors have a limited time to visit the displays.

   b. When exhibits contain items from other collections, however, many more people can see and enjoy those items.

Van Goor and Hacker, *Developmental Exercises for Rules for Writers*, 7th ed. (Boston: Bedford, 2012)

46-3 | Nouns and noun/adjectives   **159**

EXERCISE 46-4 ◆ Pronouns and pronoun/adjectives

To read about this topic, see section 46b in *Rules for Writers*, Seventh Edition.

A Circle the five pronouns in each group of six words. Example:

(his)　(they)　under　(whoever)　(no one)　(themselves)

1. I	she	of	he	ours	everyone
2. her	me	it	to	whose	many
3. for	him	you	us	this	someone
4. they	my	that	we	from	some
5. in	them	mine	your	these	nothing
6. at	yours	her	his	all	none
7. hers	our	its	nobody	another	over
8. under	myself	their	yours	each	several
9. from	theirs	who	which	either	something
10. whom	those	any	both	few	through

B Underline the pronouns (including pronoun/adjectives) in the following sentences. Except in the example, there are two in each sentence. Example:

Our Declaration of Independence includes these famous words: "We hold these truths to be self-evident."

11. Whoever reads the Declaration of Independence finds a message for everyone.

12. One of its basic premises is the equality of people.

13. Furthermore, the Declaration declares, "They are endowed by their Creator with certain unalienable rights."

14. "Among these are life, liberty, and the pursuit of happiness" may be its most famous line.

15. Refugees who apply for citizenship are claiming those rights.

Van Goor and Hacker, *Developmental Exercises for Rules for Writers*, 7th ed. (Boston: Bedford, 2012)

EXERCISE 46-5 ◆ Verbs

To read about this topic, see section 46c in *Rules for Writers*, Seventh Edition.

A | All of the following paired sentences contain some form of the word *promise*. In each pair, circle the letter of the sentence that uses a form of the word *promise* as a verb. (Hint: The words *promised* and *promising* can sometimes function as adjectives.) Example:

a. The founders of this country made certain promises to one another.

(b.) Each document of this country promises special things to the people who live here.

1. a. In a way, the Constitution is a set of promises.

   b. The government promises to do certain things for citizens.

2. a. In turn, the citizens must promise to obey certain laws.

   b. The citizens' promise is just as important as the government's.

3. a. Some early citizens thought the Constitution had not promised them enough rights.

   b. They thought that the promised rights were not specific enough.

4. a. By adding a Bill of Rights to the Constitution, citizens demanded a promise about freedom of religion.

   b. The Bill of Rights does indeed promise freedom of religion.

5. a. One of the most promising signs of political health in the colonies was their insistence on gaining certain rights.

   b. Whenever citizens repeat their oath of allegiance, they are promising anew to honor the Constitution.

B | Underline all verbs in the following paragraph and label them MV (main verb) or HV (helping verb). The first sentence has been done for you.

       HV   MV

Who should vote? All citizens should go to the polls and vote. When citizens do this, they are making important choices that can affect their lives and the lives of others. In addition, citizens must tell their elected representatives how they feel about certain issues. If the representatives ignore these messages, they may lose their jobs. It is important that these representatives stay in touch with the voters, but it is just as important that the voters send messages. Without this kind of communication, America's great democratic experiment will fail.

Van Goor and Hacker, *Developmental Exercises for Rules for Writers*, 7th ed. (Boston: Bedford, 2012)

46-5 | Verbs **161**

EXERCISE 46-6 ◆ Adjectives and adverbs

To read about this topic, see sections 46d and 46e in *Rules for Writers*, Seventh Edition.

A Label each of the following words as an adjective (ADJ) or an adverb (ADV). You should find twelve adjectives and eight adverbs. Example:

clean ___ADJ___

1. inexpensive _____
2. very _____
3. rude _____
4. not _____
5. crazy _____
6. lovely _____
7. extremely _____

8. beautiful _____
9. sometimes _____
10. political _____
11. ten _____
12. never _____
13. tired _____
14. aloud _____

15. rich _____
16. lonely _____
17. oily _____
18. slowly _____
19. always _____
20. common _____

B Label the adjectives (ADJ) and adverbs (ADV) in the following sentences. Ignore the articles *a, an,* and *the.* You should find ten adjectives and five adverbs. Example:

                                    ADJ   *ADV*   *ADJ*

The Constitution and the Bill of Rights are separate, but they go together as a single

document.

21. The Bill of Rights consists of the ten amendments that immediately follow the Constitution.

22. The First Amendment is the most familiar of the famous rights.

23. It guarantees religious freedom and freedom of speech for American citizens.

24. It also guarantees freedom of the press, an extremely important freedom in a democratic

    country.

25. Because representatives to the original Congress valued the right to discuss legislation

    publicly, the Bill of Rights assures citizens of the right to hold meetings and to petition the

    federal government.

Van Goor and Hacker, *Developmental Exercises for Rules for Writers,* 7th ed. (Boston: Bedford, 2012)

EXERCISE 46-7 ◆ Prepositions

To read about this topic, see section 46f in *Rules for Writers*, Seventh Edition.

A Many prepositions express opposite ideas. Fill in the following blanks with prepositions that express the opposite idea to the one listed. Examples:

like ___*unlike*___   into ___*out of*___

1. above _____   6. after _____

2. against _____   7. down _____

3. in _____   8. inside _____

4. on _____   9. over _____

5. to _____   10. with _____

B Circle all twenty prepositions in the following paragraph.

The men who wrote the Declaration of Independence dealt with many political controversies. In addition, they disagreed about many ideas. During their discussions, some felt they should come to terms with England, some wanted to give all of the reasons for their break with England, and some were against war under the existing circumstances. They argued over these issues frequently, making agreement seem impossible at first. They stuck to their task despite many disagreements among individuals, and in the end they put their thoughts into words that have remained famous to future generations.

Van Goor and Hacker, *Developmental Exercises for
Rules for Writers*, 7th ed. (Boston: Bedford, 2012)

46-7 | Prepositions   **163**

EXERCISE 46-8 ◆ Prepositions and conjunctions

To read about this topic, see sections 46f and 46g in *Rules for Writers*, Seventh Edition.

In the following sentences, label all prepositions (P), coordinating conjunctions (CC), and subordinating conjunctions (SUB). The numbers in the brackets after each sentence indicate how many of each you should find. Example:

> *SUB*   *P*   *P*   *CC*
> **When the Bill of Rights was adopted, it gave to American citizens rights and guarantees**
>   *P*   *CC*
> **none of the colonists or their predecessors had enjoyed. [3P, 2CC, 1SUB]**

1. When the founders of the United States wrote the Bill of Rights, they were recalling their past troubles with England. [3P, 1SUB]

2. They were also hoping that this new country and its laws would be different. [1CC, 1SUB]

3. Before the American Revolution, English officers and their men had been quartered in colonists' homes. [2P, 1CC]

4. The colonists often objected, but they could do nothing about the situation. [1P, 1CC]

5. Although they petitioned and appealed, nothing changed. [1CC, 1SUB]

6. Because the colonists objected to this practice, they put a special amendment about it in the Bill of Rights. [4P, 1SUB]

7. That amendment says that the government cannot make people give free room and board to soldiers unless the country is at war. [2P, 1CC, 2SUB]

8. Another problem was that, although the colonists objected, under English rule they and their homes could be searched by any magistrate or his appointees. [2P, 2CC, 2SUB]

9. Another amendment to the Bill of Rights would protect citizens from unreasonable searches; searching a citizen's home would require a warrant. [3P]

10. Because the Bill of Rights was added to the Constitution, Americans are still protected from these and several other intrusions by the government. [4P, 1CC, 1SUB]

Van Goor and Hacker, *Developmental Exercises for Rules for Writers*, 7th ed. (Boston: Bedford, 2012)

EXERCISE 46-9 ◆ Parts of speech: Review

To read about this topic, see section 46 in *Rules for Writers*, Seventh Edition.

In the following paragraphs, label the parts of speech of the italicized words using these codes: noun (N), pronoun (PN), helping verb (HV), main verb (MV), adjective (ADJ), adverb (ADV), preposition (P), conjunction (C). The first word has been labeled for you.

                                              ADJ

Americans fought a long *hard* war to secure the freedoms and rights that *their* Declaration proclaimed. Even *while* the war was going on, France (America's ally) *was* trying to get America to agree *to* a truce. France proposed a treaty that *would* give America its independence *without* any questions. But under the French *proposal*, the boundaries of America would be established *by* which country's army was *currently* in control of the land. That would give Spain *and* France control of major portions *of* the land Americans claimed. John Adams, America's *negotiator*, refused to discuss such a plan.

Adams was simply carrying out the spirit of the Declaration that had started the war. In the final *section* of their Declaration of Independence, the Americans had *used* another impossibly long sentence—more than one hundred words—to declare their separation from Great Britain and their determination to make their own decisions. They could *not* have known then how *costly* defending that Declaration would be. *But* when the war was over, the colonists had won the rights for which *they* had pledged their lives, their fortunes, and their *sacred* honor.

Van Goor and Hacker, *Developmental Exercises for Rules for Writers*, 7th ed. (Boston: Bedford, 2012)

46-9 | Parts of speech: Review   **165**

EXERCISE 47-1 ◆ Sentence patterns: Preview

To read about this topic, see section 47 in *Rules for Writers*, Seventh Edition.

Label the function of each italicized word or word group in the following paragraphs. Use these codes: subject (S), verb (V), subject complement (SC), direct object (DO), indirect object (IO), and object complement (OC). The first sentence has been labeled for you; answers to this exercise appear in the back of this book.

New art *forms* often *lead* the *public* to a new way of looking at things. Frequently, however, viewers are not yet ready to understand the new forms.

A *group* of French artists *had* this *problem* in the 1800s. These artists completely changed their way of painting. Instead of painting in the subdued, dark tones of a formal studio, *they* often *went* outdoors. One of their new techniques was the use of color. *They* nearly always *gave* their *paintings* great *bursts* of color, like sunlight on a field. Art *lovers* in France *were surprised* by such bright colors on the artists' canvases. People often called such paintings "open-air paintings." These *artists* usually *made* even their indoor *scenes* very *bright* with light and colors. Through an open window onto a bouquet of flowers or a bright-haired child *would pour* bright *sunshine*. *Were* Pierre-Auguste Renoir's *paintings* always *bright* and *cheerful*? Yes, and those of Claude Monet, Camille Pissarro, and Paul Cézanne were equally pleasant. These *painters*, now called "impressionists," *are admired* all over the world today, but in their own time the artists had to educate their viewers.

Twentieth-century artists had the same problem. Two new art *forms* from that period *are* good *examples*, "op art" and "pop art." *Both* of these *showed* their *viewers* everyday *objects* in quite different ways. Both eventually attracted a following. But like many artists before them, the op-art and pop-art painters had to educate their viewers first.

Van Goor and Hacker, *Developmental Exercises for Rules for Writers*, 7th ed. (Boston: Bedford, 2012)

EXERCISE 47-2 ◆ Subjects

To read about this topic, see section 47 in *Rules for Writers*, Seventh Edition.

A Each of the following sentences has three words or word groups italicized. One of these words or word groups is the subject. Find it and label it S. Example:

> *S*
> Many *artists* have *preferred* certain colors for their *work*.

1. During one *part* of his life, *Picasso* preferred the color *blue*.

2. *There* are many famous *paintings* by Picasso from *this* period.

3. "*Blue*" refers not only to the predominant *color* of these paintings but also to their *mood*.

4. In these paintings *you* will find *outcasts* or victims of *society* as the main characters.

5. Do the *derelicts and beggars* in these pictures reflect *Picasso's* own sense of *isolation*?

B In the following paragraph, complete subjects have been italicized. Label the simple subject (or subjects) SS. The first sentence has been labeled for you.

> *SS*   *SS*
Pierre-Auguste Renoir and his young friends founded a new movement called "impressionism." Instead of trying to reproduce a scene exactly, *impressionist painters like Renoir and his friends* blended small brushstrokes of different colors to give a general impression of a scene. Up close, *a careful observer of a restaurant scene* sees no solid edges on a table or a lady's hat, just small dabs of paint. At a distance, however, *that same careful observer* will clearly see the picture in the artist's mind. At first *the art world* laughed at and rejected the new movement. However, there is now *no serious argument about the importance of the impressionist movement*.

Van Goor and Hacker, *Developmental Exercises for
Rules for Writers*, 7th ed. (Boston: Bedford, 2012)

47-2 | Subjects **167**

EXERCISE 47-3 ◆ Direct objects and subject complements

To read about this topic, see section 47b in *Rules for Writers*, Seventh Edition.

A Subjects and verbs have been labeled in the following sentences. Label each italicized word as a simple direct object (DO) or a simple subject complement (SC). Example:

> s   v   SC
> **Pierre-Auguste Renoir's parents were *supportive* of their son's ambitions.**

1.   s   v
    Renoir's love of art was *clear* to his parents.

2.   s v   s   v
    When he was a *boy* of thirteen, they apprenticed *him* to a porcelain artist.

3.   s   v
    Renoir first learned the potter's *trade*.

4.   s v
    Soon he was quite *skillful* at making and firing vases.

5.   s   v
    He enjoyed the *task* of decorating the vases even more.

B Using the pattern of each sentence as a model, write a short sentence of your own on any subject. Example:

S/V/SC: Renoir was an artist.

Casey was a ballplayer. _____

6.   S/V: Renoir studied.

_____

7.   S/V: Renoir studied hard.

_____

8.   S/V/SC: He became an excellent painter.

_____

9.   S/V/SC: His paintings are cheerful.

_____

10. S/V/DO: Café owners liked his murals.

_____

Van Goor and Hacker, *Developmental Exercises for Rules for Writers*, 7th ed. (Boston: Bedford, 2012)

EXERCISE 47-4 ◆ Indirect objects and object complements

To read about this topic, see section 47b in *Rules for Writers*, Seventh Edition.

A Subjects, verbs, and direct objects are labeled in the following sentences. Label each italicized word as a simple indirect object (IO) or a simple object complement (OC). Example:

          S   V   *IO*   DO

Renoir's parents gave *him* a good start in his chosen profession.

                               S   V   DO

1. Besides his parents, other people considered the young Renoir a fine *painter*.

    S ┌——V——┐   DO

2. He had shown local *businessmen* some of his work.

     S   V   DO

3. Owners of some Paris cafés gave *him* painting jobs.

     S   V   DO

4. He made the walls of their cafés *beautiful*.

           S   V   ┌———DO———┐

5. The lovely scenes made both customers and owners *happy*.

B Using the pattern of each sentence as a model, write a short sentence of your own on any subject. Example:

S/V/DO/OC: Renoir called his style of painting "impressionist."

Casey called his style of batting "the best."
_____

6. S/V/IO/DO: Paris café owners offered Renoir much work.

_____

7. S/V/IO/DO: They gave him twenty orders for murals.

_____

8. S/V/DO/OC: They considered his work exceptional.

_____

9. S/V/DO/OC: People called him "the happy painter."

_____

10. S/V: His popularity increased.

_____

Van Goor and Hacker, *Developmental Exercises for Rules for Writers*, 7th ed. (Boston: Bedford, 2012)

47-4 | Indirect objects and object complements **169**

EXERCISE 47-5 ◆ Direct objects, indirect objects, and object complements

To read about this topic, see section 47b in *Rules for Writers*, Seventh Edition.

Underline the verb of each sentence. Then label the complete direct object (DO) and any complete indirect objects (IO) or object complements (OC). Example:

┌─DO─┐   ┌──────DO──────┐ ┌──────OC──────┐
Many people <u>enjoy</u> pop art. They <u>find</u> this new kind of art a refreshing change.

1. During World War II, American mass media flooded London.

2. The effect of that flood fascinated many London artists.

3. Using the American material, British artists gave the world a new art form.

4. To produce their art, the artists used images from popular culture.

5. Someone named the new art "pop art."

6. Most Americans find pop art very appealing.

7. To some, it reflects the optimism of the 1960s.

8. Items like flags, signs, and comic strips gave pop artists their subject matter.

9. Artists like Jasper Johns and Roy Lichtenstein preceded the more famous Andy Warhol.

10. Of all these artists, Andy Warhol best understood the media's power to affect people's thinking.

Van Goor and Hacker, *Developmental Exercises for Rules for Writers*, 7th ed. (Boston: Bedford, 2012)

EXERCISE 47-6 ◆ Sentence patterns: Review

To read about this topic, see section 47 in *Rules for Writers*, Seventh Edition.

Label the function of each italicized word or word group in the following paragraph using these codes: subject (S), verb (V), subject complement (SC), direct object (DO), indirect object (IO), and object complement (OC). The first sentence has been labeled for you.

            S   *V*   *DO*

     Renoir definitely *had* firm *ideas* about work and about getting along with people. As for work, he believed that *people* everywhere *should use* their *hands* every day. He certainly did, and because he did, *friends* often *called* this hardworking *man* a *workman-painter*. Being called a workman-painter pleased Renoir. Work seemed to be more important to him than the finished product. "The only *reward* for work *is* the *work* itself," he said. He got along with people very well; even his enemies seemed to like him. When his opponents attacked his views, *he* frequently *responded* by suggesting a compromise. *He* freely *offered* other *people* his own successful *techniques* for getting along with his opponents. According to Renoir, *you* certainly *should give* your *enemies* a *chance*. You should also avoid a fight whenever possible. Why? If you avoid fights, your *enemies* often *will become* your *friends*. The *joy* in Renoir's paintings *might be explained* by these approaches to life.

Van Goor and Hacker, *Developmental Exercises for Rules for Writers*, 7th ed. (Boston: Bedford, 2012)

47-6 | Sentence patterns: Review   **171**

EXERCISE 48-1 ◆ Subordinate word groups: Preview

To read about this topic, see section 48 in *Rules for Writers*, Seventh Edition.

In the following paragraphs, underline prepositional and verbal phrases once; underline subordinate clauses twice. The first sentence has been done for you; you should find fourteen phrases and five subordinate clauses. Answers to this exercise appear in the back of this book.

Louise Nevelson, who was once called "the finest living American artist," did not earn that title easily.

From her earliest years, she was artistically inclined. Drawing colorful pictures was a favorite childhood pastime. To decorate her room, she collected boxes of pretty rocks, shells, and fabric pieces. Encouraging her artistic interest, her family gave her the independence that she needed.

Her husband, Charles Nevelson, who was a wealthy New York businessman, gave her financial independence, but Louise Nevelson needed personal independence too. The marriage lasted for only eleven years. Then she and her son, Mike, went to her family home. Mike stayed there while his mother studied abroad. Studying, working, and making new friends, Louise developed the self-confidence to follow her own vision.

At times she must have wondered whether she had done the right thing. During Louise Nevelson's busiest and most exciting years, her paintings and sculptures were not popular with either the critics or the public. Later, however, her work won critical acclaim, and she was recognized throughout the art world. Rewarded and acclaimed, Louise Nevelson knew that she had made the right decision.

Van Goor and Hacker, *Developmental Exercises for Rules for Writers*, 7th ed. (Boston: Bedford, 2012)

EXERCISE 48-2 ◆ Prepositional phrases

To read about this topic, see section 48a in *Rules for Writers*, Seventh Edition.

Underline the twenty prepositional phrases in the following sentences. Example:

> **Children learn many things <u>from their parents</u>.**

1. From her builder-father, Louise Nevelson learned an important tradition that had been handed down for generations.

2. Like many other Jewish traditions, it is recorded in the Talmud.

3. The Talmud is a book about Jewish history and laws; it is studied by Jewish scholars.

4. According to the Talmud, Jews should always leave some part of a new house unfinished or unpainted.

5. The unfinished part is there for a reason: It makes people remember the destruction of Jerusalem's Second Temple.

6. As an adult, Louise moved into a dozen or more "new homes."

7. Sometimes she abided by the tradition, but sometimes she forgot about it.

8. Finally, she understood at last this tradition that had been handed down for all those years.

9. She saw that over the years she had often left some work unfinished in her studio.

10. Both her work and her life were like her house: Only with an unfinished corner could they grow and change.

Van Goor and Hacker, *Developmental Exercises for Rules for Writers*, 7th ed. (Boston: Bedford, 2012)

48-2 | Prepositional phrases **173**

EXERCISE 48-3 ◆ Prepositional and verbal phrases

To read about this topic, see sections 48a and 48b in *Rules for Writers*, Seventh Edition.

Some of the phrases in the following paragraphs are italicized. Label these phrases prepositional (PR), gerund (G), infinitive (I), or participial (PT). The first one has been labeled for you.

Louise Nevelson's first one-woman show came about because Nevelson was determined
$$I$$
to have her work recognized. Her first choice of a showplace was the Nierendorf Gallery.

Exhibiting there would put her in the same place where Picasso, Matisse, and Paul Klee had been

exhibited. *Showing New York City's best modern art* had helped build a strong reputation for this

gallery.

Nevelson went alone to the gallery. First she found Mr. Nierendorf, the gallery's manager.

Then, *introducing herself quickly,* she stated quite simply that she wanted an exhibition in his

gallery. He was surprised at her forthrightness, but he was also impressed. When he protested that

he did not know her work, Nevelson simply invited him *to come and see it.*

He did—the next day—and he offered her a show in twenty-one days. *During the next*

weeks, Nevelson got her pieces ready. When the show opened, it was Nierendorf's first exhibition *of*

an American artist.

With a few exceptions, art critics liked the show. *Excited by her work,* one critic said that he

would have "hailed these sculptural expressions as by surely a great figure among moderns"—if

he had not found out the artist was a woman. That left-handed compliment did more harm to

the critic than to the artist. Other critics, *seeing similar forms and rhythms,* compared her work

favorably to Mayan work. Still others commented on the work's "wit" and "zest" and "interest in

movement."

Received very well, the exhibition was extended past its closing date and gave Nevelson

opportunities *to meet some important people*—but not a single piece of art was sold.

Van Goor and Hacker, *Developmental Exercises for Rules for Writers,* 7th ed. (Boston: Bedford, 2012)

EXERCISE 48-4 ◆ Verbal phrases

To read about this topic, see section 48b in *Rules for Writers*, Seventh Edition.

The verbal phrase in each of the following sentences has been italicized. Label these phrases gerund (G), participial (PT), or infinitive (I). Example:

> *G*
> ***Working with other artists*** **made Louise Nevelson very happy.**

1. *Enjoying one another's company*, the members of Ben Shahn's artist group often ate dinner together at a restaurant.

2. Frequently, they would paint a picture right then and there *to celebrate their joy*.

3. *Needing the white tablecloth for their canvas*, the artists would push aside the dishes and food.

4. *Totally involved in their project*, they would look for "paint."

5. *Finding something to use for paint* was not usually a problem.

6. *Making paint from wine drops or pepper or anything else handy* gave them pleasure.

7. Each artist had a chance *to add to the picture*.

8. They enjoyed *adding details to the other artists' parts of the picture*.

9. *Relaxed and refreshed*, they would leave the restaurant content.

10. No one knows why the restaurant owner allowed them *to do this repeatedly to his tablecloths*!

Van Goor and Hacker, *Developmental Exercises for Rules for Writers*, 7th ed. (Boston: Bedford, 2012)

48-4 | Verbal phrases **175**

EXERCISE 48-5 ♦ Subordinate clauses

To read about this topic, see section 48e in *Rules for Writers*, Seventh Edition.

A Underline the subordinate clauses in the following sentences. Example:

When Louise was part of a struggling young artists' group in New York, she met Diego Rivera.

1. Diego Rivera, who was a Mexican mural painter, introduced Louise Nevelson to other artists and their friends.

2. One of the people she met, Marjorie Eaton, became her roommate.

3. Louise also met Ben Shahn while she was working with Rivera.

4. When Louise began working with Ben, she felt at ease with her art for the first time.

5. She knew that she had found her niche.

B Identify each of the following word groups as a prepositional phrase or a subordinate clause. Example:

a.	After work	*prepositional phrase*
b.	After she had worked	*subordinate clause*

6.	a.	Before she went to class	_____
	b.	Before her painting class	_____
7.	a.	Since her happy childhood days	_____
	b.	Since she had a happy childhood	_____
8.	a.	Till the closing bell	_____
	b.	Till the bell rang	_____
9.	a.	After the mural was done	_____
	b.	After the sculpture show	_____
10.	a.	Until she mastered the skill	_____
	b.	Until her first exhibition	_____

Van Goor and Hacker, *Developmental Exercises for Rules for Writers*, 7th ed. (Boston: Bedford, 2012)

EXERCISE 48-6 ◆ Subordinate word groups: Review

To read about this topic, see section 48 in *Rules for Writers*, Seventh Edition.

In the following paragraphs, underline prepositional and verbal phrases once; underline subordinate clauses twice. The first sentence has been done for you; you should find twenty more subordinate word groups.

Perhaps becoming a queen is one of every little girl's fantasies. During one experimental stage, Louise Nevelson gave herself that title. She called herself "Queen of the Black Black." While she was experimenting, she used only black materials in her artwork. She decided to make all her surroundings black also. Painting her walls black was the first step. Then she attacked the floors. She did not want to paint them; instead, she used stain to get the desired effect. Stained very dark, the floors did not reflect much light. Her work used no other color, and she insisted that black was "the total color."

At fifty-eight, Louise Nevelson was finally recognized. She became an artist who could expect regular exhibits, sales, and commissions. Museums and collectors bought her work eagerly, paying her well. She was awarded honorary degrees from various universities and accepted invitations to attend White House dinners. She enjoyed receiving these honors, but her greatest pleasure came later.

When Louise Nevelson celebrated her eightieth birthday, her hometown gave her what she had always wanted: The local museum exhibited her work, and the town bestowed a title upon her—"Queen of the City."

Van Goor and Hacker, *Developmental Exercises for Rules for Writers*, 7th ed. (Boston: Bedford, 2012)

48-6 | Subordinate word groups: Review   **177**

EXERCISE 49-1 ♦ Sentence types: Preview

To read about this topic, see section 49 in *Rules for Writers*, Seventh Edition.

In the following paragraphs, indicate on the blank space after each sentence whether the sentence is simple (S), compound (C), complex (CX), or compound-complex (CC). Two blanks have been filled for you; answers to this exercise appear in the back of this book.

Most Americans of any age recognize the name Jackie Robinson. _____ Even if they are not sports fans, Americans know some basic facts about him. _____ Jackie Robinson played baseball, he was good at it, and he was the first black man on a major league team. ___*C*___ Even more important than what Jackie Robinson did on the ball field is what he did off the field. _____

Several off-the-field incidents occurred when he was in the army during World War II. ____*CX*____ His sports prowess was well known, and he was avidly recruited for both football and baseball teams. _____ Because the football team was not integrated, Robinson refused to play on any army team. _____ While he was still in the army—and a second lieutenant to boot— the driver of the bus taking soldiers from the base into town ordered Robinson to go to the back of the bus. _____ (In those days in the southern states, the front and middle sections of a bus were for whites only.) _____ Robinson knew his rights as a soldier; when he refused to go to the back, he was arrested. _____ When his case came up, Robinson defended himself in the military court and won. _____

These off-the-field incidents foreshadowed important events that followed. _____

Van Goor and Hacker, *Developmental Exercises for Rules for Writers*, 7th ed. (Boston: Bedford, 2012)

EXERCISE 49-2 ◆ Sentence types

To read about this topic, see section 49 in *Rules for Writers*, Seventh Edition.

In the following sentences, underline any subordinate clauses. Then determine the sentence type and indicate it in the blank: simple, compound, complex, or compound-complex. (Hint: Some sentences do not have a subordinate clause.) Example:

In 1945, Branch Rickey was president and general manager of the Brooklyn Dodgers.

_simple_____

1. Driven by his ambition to build America's strongest baseball team, Rickey wanted the best talent in the world. _____

2. Believing also that keeping nonwhites out of baseball was morally wrong, he had been studying the players in the Negro leagues. _____

3. He needed someone who was as good off the field as on the field. _____

4. The Negro leagues had plenty of good players, and Rickey's scouts watched them all, reporting on each one. _____

5. Impressed by the reports on Robinson's family life and by his postponement of marriage until he had a job, Rickey wanted to meet this ballplayer. _____

6. Reports also showed Robinson's fiery temper; worried, Rickey flew Robinson to New York for an interview. _____

7. In the interview, Rickey taunted Robinson with snide remarks and mean insults, making it quite clear that Robinson's ability to deal with such things—on and off the field—was as important as his ability to play ball. _____

8. Robinson understood: He could not lose his temper on the field or off, he could not respond in kind even if he was physically attacked, and he had to maintain this nonviolent stance for at least three years. _____

9. It was not a role that Robinson was used to; did he have the self-control to carry that role?

   _____

10. Robinson decided that he did, and the two men shook hands. _____

Van Goor and Hacker, *Developmental Exercises for Rules for Writers*, 7th ed. (Boston: Bedford, 2012)

49-2 | Sentence types **179**

EXERCISE 49-3 ◆ Sentence types: Review

To read about this topic, see section 49 in *Rules for Writers*, Seventh Edition.

Indicate on the blank after each sentence in the following paragraphs whether the sentence is simple (S), compound (C), complex (CX), or compound-complex (CC). One of each kind has been labeled for you.

Robinson very quickly had a chance to test his commitment to nonviolence; on the way to training camp in Florida, he and his bride were bumped from flights and refused service in the coffee shop. ____*C*____ When they finally got to Florida, they rode a segregated bus to get to Daytona Beach. _____ At training camp, white players stayed in nice hotels and ate in hotel dining rooms; Robinson and other blacks had to find homes or motels in the black community and eat in black restaurants. _____ Robinson kept his temper, diverting his anger into the force with which he handled the ball and bat. _____

The story best remembered about Jackie Robinson is probably the one involving Pee Wee Reese, a southerner on the team. ____*S*____ Some fans at a Cincinnati game yelled that he should not be playing with a black man, and Reese pretended not to hear. _____ He walked up to Robinson on first base, put a hand on his shoulder, and began a conversation. _____ Later, neither man could remember what they had talked about—but the fans understood Pee Wee's gesture and settled down. ____*CC*____

In his baseball career, Jackie Robinson broke many records and won many awards. _____ In 1962, he was inducted into the Baseball Hall of Fame—the first African American to be so recognized. _____ He was recognized outside the sports world as well, his top honor being the Presidential Medal of Freedom. _____ Again, what he did off the field was even more important than what he did on it. _____

Today, the Jackie Robinson Foundation provides education and opportunities for young people who, in turn, give back to the community. _____ Since its formation in 1973, it has encouraged and supported thousands of young people who commit to lifelong engagement in their own worlds, who understand the importance of their off-the-field lives. ____*CX*____

Van Goor and Hacker, *Developmental Exercises for Rules for Writers*, 7th ed. (Boston: Bedford, 2012)

Answers to Guided Practice and Preview Exercises

EXERCISE 8-1, page 1

Suggested revision:

Young slave Frederick Douglass enjoyed indulging in his favorite fantasy about slave owners. In his fantasy, everyone conspired against the slave owners. Slaves still in bondage gave no hint of a planned escape. Members of the community never revealed the whereabouts of escaped slaves. Slaves who escaped successfully never talked too much about how they got away. Recaptured slaves told their owners nothing at all. Even some white southerners who sympathized with the slaves gave no information to their slave-owning friends. Douglass enjoyed the final part of his fantasy most. In it, Douglass imagined slave owners as being too afraid to hunt escaping slaves. The owners distrusted their slaves, their enemies, and even their friends.

EXERCISE 9-1, page 5

Suggested revision:

In his own time, one famous sixteenth-century Italian was known only by his given name, Leonardo. Today he is still known by that single name. But then and now, his name suggests many different roles: biologist, botanist, inventor, engineer, strategist, researcher, and artist.

Sixteenth-century Venetian soldiers knew Leonardo as a military strategist. When the Turkish fleet was invading their country, Leonardo suggested conducting surprise underwater attacks and flooding the land that the Turkish army had to cross. Engineers knew him as the man who laid out new canals for the city of Milan. Scientists admired him not only for his precise anatomical drawings but also for his discovery that hardening of the arteries could cause death. To Milan's royal court, Leonardo was the artist who was painting impressive portraits, sculpting a bronze horse memorial to the house of Sforza, and at the same time working on a mural of the Last Supper.

Leonardo saw a three-dimensional *s*-curve in all of nature—the flow of water, the movements of animals, and the flight of birds. We recognize the same *s*-curve today in the spiraling form of DNA. Leonardo invented the wave theory: He saw that grain bending as the wind blew over it and water rippling from a stone dropped into it were the same scientific event. It was as easy for him to see this wave in sound and light as to observe it in fields and streams. The math of his day could not explain all his theories, but twentieth-century scientists showed the world that Leonardo knew what he was talking about.

Leonardo saw very clearly that the powers of nature could be destructive and that human beings could be savage. At the same time, he saw a unity holding all of life's varied parts together, a unity he could express in his art.

Leonardo—it's quite a name!

EXERCISE 10-1, page 9

Suggested revision:

Mary Wollstonecraft, an eighteenth-century writer, may have been England's first feminist. Her entire life reflected her belief in equal rights for women in all areas of their lives: personal, intellectual, and professional.

From childhood, she never had accepted and never would accept the idea that men were superior to women. As a young girl, she knew that her drinking and gambling father deserved less respect than her long-suffering mother did. As an adult, she demanded that society give her the same freedom it gave men.

Wollstonecraft also demanded that men pay attention to her ideas. She did not argue about an idea. Instead, she gave an example of what she objected to and invited her readers to think about it from various points of view. Working this way, she made few enemies among intellectuals. Indeed, she was attracted to and respected by some of the leading intellectuals of her day. Among them she was as well known on one side of the Atlantic as on the other. Thomas Paine, the American orator and writer, probably knew her better than Samuel Johnson, the English writer, did.

Professionally, she was a governess, a teacher, and an author. When her father's drinking destroyed the family, she and her sisters started a girls' school. Eventually, financial problems forced the school to close, but not before Mary had acquired enough firsthand experience to write *Thoughts on the Education of Daughters* (1786). As competent as or more competent than other writers of the day, she was a more persuasive advocate for women than most other writers were.

Modern feminists may find it ironic that current encyclopedia entries for "Wollstonecraft" refer researchers to "Godwin," her married name—where they will find her entry longer than the entry for her famous husband, William Godwin.

EXERCISE 11-1, page 13

Suggested revision:

Sometimes it's hard to separate history from folklore. Casey Jones, John Henry, Johnny Appleseed, Uncle Sam—which of these were real men? We've heard their stories, but are those stories true?

There really was a railroad engineer called Casey Jones; he got that nickname because of Cayce, Kentucky, where he lived as a boy. There really was a Cannonball too; it was the Illinois Central's fast mail and passenger train. There really was a wreck of Engine No. 382, and Casey died while slowing the train to save his passengers. Legend has it that when workers found his body in the wreckage, his hand was still on the air-brake lever. (Air brakes had recently been installed on trains to increase their braking power.)

John Henry was an African American railroad worker of great strength. In legend and song, he died after a timed contest against a steam drill. By using a hammer in each hand, John Henry won the contest. He drilled two holes seven feet deep; the steam drill bored only one nine-foot hole. The real John Henry died on the job, crushed by rocks that fell from the ceiling of a railroad tunnel.

John Chapman, better known as Johnny Appleseed, was a wealthy and well-liked nurseryman who kept moving his place of business west as the frontier moved west. His boyhood friend Sam Wilson supplied meat to the US troops during the War of 1812. A worker told a government inspector that the "US" stamped on the meat stood for "Uncle Sam." Although it was a joke, it caught on, and Congress made the "Uncle Sam" identification official in the 1960s.

EXERCISE 12-1, page 17

Suggested revision:

Hearing the name Karl Marx, people usually think first of Russia. Marx never lived in Russia at all. Actually, he spent almost all of his adult life in England. He was a political exile for the last half of his life.

Marx lived first in Germany. Born of Jewish parents, he completed his university studies with a PhD at the University of Jena. His favorite professor tried to get Marx an appointment to teach at the university. When that professor was fired, Marx gave up hope of teaching at Jena or any other German university. Because he was denied a university position, Marx had to earn his living as a journalist. He worked briefly as a newspaper editor in Germany.

Next came France, Belgium, and a return to Germany. First Marx and his new bride moved to Paris, where Marx worked for a radical journal and became friendly with Friedrich Engels. When the journal ceased publication, Marx moved to Brussels, Belgium, and then back to Cologne, Germany. He did not hold a regular job, so he tried desperately to earn at least enough money to feed his family.

After living in Paris and Brussels, Marx decided he would settle in London. He and his family lived in abject poverty while Marx earned what little income he could by writing for an American newspaper, the *New York Tribune*.

EXERCISE 13-1, page 21

Suggested revision:

Do you know how slavery began in America or how it ended? When the *Mayflower* landed in what is now Massachusetts in September 1620, slaves were already in America. A Dutch ship had unloaded and sold twenty Africans in Jamestown, Virginia, the year before.

Actually, slavery in America began long before that. Many early explorers brought slaves with them to the new land, and some historians claim that one of the men in Christopher Columbus's crew was a slave. From the 1500s to the 1800s, slave ships brought ten million African slaves across the ocean.

Most of the slaves stayed in Latin America and the West Indies, but the southern part of the United States received about 6 percent of them. Few northerners owned slaves, and opposition to slavery was evident by the time of the American Revolution. Rhode Island prohibited the importation of slaves even before the Revolutionary War. After the war, six northern states abolished slavery at once, and other states passed laws to phase out slavery; even Virginia enacted legislation encouraging slave owners to emancipate their slaves.

But it took a war, a tricky political situation, and a very clever former slave to free all slaves. History gives Abraham Lincoln the credit for liberating the slaves during the Civil War, and he deserves some credit, but emancipation was not his idea. Originally, no government officials seriously considered emancipation because they were so focused on winning the war to save the Union. Then an important black man talked to Lincoln and gave him the idea and the reason. This man said that freeing slaves would be good for the war effort and asked if Lincoln would agree to do it. Who was this man? He was Frederick Douglass, fugitive slave and newspaper editor.

EXERCISE 14-1, page 25

Suggested revision:

No one who knew Albert Einstein as a young child would ever have believed that he might one day be called the smartest man in the world. None of his teachers could have predicted success for him. A shy, slow learner, Albert always got into trouble in class. He consistently failed the subjects he did not like. His family could not have predicted his success either. Albert could not even get to meals on time. Night after night his parents had to postpone dinner until servants searched the house and grounds and found the boy. He would be full of apologies but have no explanation to offer for his lateness except that he was "thinking." Once his angry father dangled his big gold watch at Albert and told him to figure out how late he was. Albert, who could not tell time, was fascinated by the tiny magnetic compass hanging from the watch chain. The boy asked so many questions about the compass that he did not eat much dinner anyway. When Albert begged his father to lend him the compass to sleep with, his father let him borrow it. Years later Einstein wondered whether that little compass had been the beginning of his interest in science.

EXERCISE 15-1, page 29

Suggested revision:

Everyone has heard of Martin Luther King Jr. After studying for the ministry at Boston University and earning a doctorate in theology, he went home to the South to work as a minister. He started working in civil rights and became the most influential leader of that cause in America. When he died, the victim of an assassin's bullet, his name was almost synonymous with "civil rights." Historians and biographers have recorded his leadership in the fight to gain basic civil rights for all Americans. Many people who know of his civil rights work, however, are not aware of his skill as a writer. In addition to his carefully crafted and emotional speeches, King produced other important writing.

Among King's most famous writings is his "Letter from Birmingham Jail." Written to answer a statement published by eight Alabama ministers that King's work was "unwise and untimely," the letter shows King to be a man who had great patience with his critics. Eager to get these ministers to accept his point of view, King reminds them that they are ministers. Their goodwill, he says, should help them see that his views hold value. Instead of attacking them personally, he analyzes their arguments and then presents his own views. Does he use many of the emotional appeals for which he is justly famous? No, in this letter King depends on logic and reasoning as the tools to win his argument.

EXERCISE 16-1, page 33

Suggested revision:

Adam Smith, the founder of modern economics, proposed a theory in the eighteenth century that has made him controversial ever since. This economist, born in Scotland and educated in England, wrote the first complete study of political economy. *The Wealth of Nations* was published in the same year that Americans declared their independence from England—1776. Smith's book pointed out the interdependence of freedom and order, economic processes, and free-trade laws. Although Smith's thinking did not really affect economic policies significantly during his lifetime, its influence in the next century was considerable. Among economists, the phrases "the invisible hand" and "laissez-faire" are synonymous with Smith's name. History has only made Smith's ideas more controversial. Say "Adam Smith" to conservative businesspeople, and they will smile and respond with words like "He was a good man—really understood how business works!" Say "Adam Smith" to liberal reformers, and they will grimace and mutter something like "He was an evil man—really sold the average citizen down the river." Both of these reactions are extreme, but such responses indicate that the controversy aroused by Smith's ideas is still alive.

EXERCISE 17-1, page 37

Suggested revisions:

A. In the 1800s, an Englishman named Thomas Robert Malthus became involved in economics. He was very interested in predicting how many more people would populate the world eventually and how much food would be available for them. What he figured out was frightening. He said that people kept having children faster than society could produce enough to feed them. There was no way to avoid it. Hard times and wars would kill most people. According to Malthus, famine, plagues, and even wars were necessary to eliminate some excess people so the remainder could have enough food.

B. Robert Malthus proved that population grows faster than food supplies. His thinking led him to oppose any help for poor people. He believed that by relieving the immediate problems of the poor, the government actually made it harder for people to feed their families. Malthus said that if the government subsidized their basic needs, people would only have more children, thus increasing the population even more. Then the inevitable famine or drought would have to eliminate even more people to help a few survive. Everyone from worker to supervisor was caught in the same predicament. It is no wonder that when the English historian Thomas Carlyle finished reading Malthus's theories, he pronounced economics "the dismal science."

EXERCISE 18-1, page 41

Suggested revision:

Economics is not totally dominated by men. Even in the 1800s, when Thomas Malthus and David Ricardo were the experts, one leading writer about economics was a woman, Jane Marcet. Marcet wrote for the popular press. One of her favorite topics to write about was political economy. In her book *Conversations in Political Economy*, Marcet summarized economic doctrines before 1800. Her aim was different from that of either Malthus or Ricardo. Rather than propounding a new theory of her own, she popularized theories of other people. Modern-day women have done more than write about theories that men have proposed. Some of them have taken the initiative to develop their own ideas. Carmen M. Reinhart, for example, has written influential papers on financial crises and has served in high-level positions in research and government organizations. She is just one of the increasing number of women making careers in economics.

EXERCISE 19-1, page 47

Suggested revision:

Four young Englishmen added a word to the world's vocabulary in the 1960s, a word that became synonymous with the 1960s, especially with the music of that time. That word was, of course, "Beatles." The Beatles became the most famous popular musical group of the twentieth century and have held the loyalty of many fans into the present century.

The Beatles were popular in Liverpool, England, and in Hamburg, Germany, before they came to America on tour and became world famous. Liverpool and Hamburg loved the four young men and their music. The Beatles' favorite club was the Cavern in Liverpool, where they hung out together, played day and night, and attracted many fans. A Liverpool disc jockey first called attention to them, and a Liverpool music critic and record store owner became their first manager. The disc jockey called them "fantastic," saying that they had "resurrected original rock 'n' roll." The music critic who became their manager, Brian Epstein, made them shape up as a group. Promoting them, arranging club dates for them, and badgering record companies for them, he was determined to win a recording contract for this exciting new group.

In England, the record buying led to the publicity. In America, the publicity led to the record buying. Everyone wanted copies of the original singles: "Love Me Do," "Please, Please Me," and "From Me to You." In America, audiences made so much noise that no one could hear the music. Crowds of screaming teenagers surrounded the Beatles wherever they went, determined to touch one or more of these famous music makers. Reporters observing the conduct of fans at Beatles' concerts found that they had to invent a new word to describe the wild, almost insane behavior of the fans. They called it "Beatlemania."

EXERCISE 20-1, page 53

Suggested revision:

Have you ever heard of the Wobblies? Not many people have these days. That's a shame, because they did at least two things for which they should be remembered. They probably saved the labor movement in America, and they definitely gave American folk music some of its most unforgettable songs. No one really knows how they got their nickname, but almost everyone knows a song or two that they inspired.

The Wobblies were the members of the Industrial Workers of the World (IWW), a small but militant coalition of radical labor groups. The Wobblies could not get along with the major union groups of the day; in fact, they alienated most of those groups.

Although the major unions disliked the Wobblies immensely, they learned some valuable lessons from them. The first lesson was to avoid getting involved in politics. If there was one thing the Wobblies hated more than capitalism, it was politics. The Wobblies avoided politics for one good reason: They [*or* they] believed that political affiliation caused the death of unions. What else did the major unions learn? They learned to deal realistically with workers' problems. Major unions also learned new recruiting techniques from the Wobblies. In addition, they copied the Wobblies in devoting their energy to nuts-and-bolts issues affecting the workers.

The major unions never recognized their debt to the Wobblies, but the debt was still there for historians to see. When historians began to compile the story of the American labor unions, they finally recognized the contributions of the Wobblies.

EXERCISE 21-1, page 60

convey, are, are, are, has, is, seem, enjoy, is, is

EXERCISE 22-1, page 64

Suggested revision:

Everyone has heard of Dorothy and Toto and their tornado "flight" from Kansas to Oz. Everyone also knows that the Oz adventure was pure fantasy and that it ended happily. But another girl from Kansas took real flights all around the real world. Whenever she landed safely after setting one of her many records, everyone rejoiced and sent congratulations to her. When she disappeared on her last flight, the whole world mourned. Not every pilot can claim to have that kind of following.

Neighbors knew that Amelia Earhart would not be a typical "lady." A child as curious, daring, and self-confident as Amelia was bound to stand out from her peers. When she and her sister Muriel were young, girls were supposed to play with dolls. If girls played baseball or collected worms, they were called "tomboys" and were often punished. Boys and girls even had different kinds of sleds—the girls' sleds were lightweight, impossible-to-steer box sleds.

But the Earhart family lived by its own rules. Amelia's father, whom she depended on for approval, bought Amelia the boys' sled she longed for. Many fast trips down steep hills gave Amelia a foretaste of flying with the wind in her face.

The closest Amelia came to flying was on a homemade roller coaster. She and her friends built it, using an old woodshed for the base of the ride. They started eight feet off the ground and tried to sled down the slope without falling off. No one was successful on the first attempt, but Amelia kept trying until she had a successful ride. Satisfied at last, she declared that the ride had felt "just like flying."

EXERCISE 23-1, page 68

Suggested revision:

George and Mary Jones lived in Memphis during the Civil War. They were sympathetic to the Union, but the city definitely favored the Confederates. Being caught in the middle made the war years especially hard on them. They looked forward to a much better life after the war.

At first, it seemed that they were going to have that better life. George got a job as a labor organizer, and Mary stayed at home to care for their four healthy children. Then came yellow fever. In nine months, Mary went from a happy wife and mother to a despondent widow with no children. She had to find work. Because a person must have some meaning for living, she needed work that she could care strongly about.

By 1900, Mary had become involved in union activities all over the United States. She found her calling among the coal miners and their wives, a calling she followed for the next thirty years. Making friends with the workers and outwitting private detectives, she held secret meetings to help the miners organize and plan strategy. The newspaper often reported her ability to outwit and outlast mine bosses and lawyers as well as to reawaken courage in disconsolate workers.

Mary Jones spent many nights in jail, but often her jailers did not know what to do with this attractive gray-haired woman whom the workers called "Mother." The jailers' confusion simply amused Mary, who was far more used to jail than her jailers could imagine.

EXERCISE 24-1, page 72

They, them, We, her, They, them, they, he, president's, she

EXERCISE 25-1, page 76

whom, whom, Who, whoever, whom
[*Note*: The *whom* in the last sentence may be dropped.]

EXERCISE 26-1, page 80

Novelists have often used their storytelling talents to influence people's thinking. Charles Dickens did it in nineteenth-century England. From *David Copperfield* to *Oliver Twist*, book after book depicted the plight of the poor and other really unfortunate members of society. Harriet Beecher Stowe did it in nineteenth-century America, but with hardly as many books. Her *Uncle Tom's Cabin* depicted slavery so well that the book strongly influenced antislavery sentiments in the decade before the Civil War.

Harriet Beecher Stowe considered slavery sinful and wanted her book to help end slavery quickly and peacefully. People first read parts of the novel ten years before the beginning of the war. An abolitionist magazine published the book a few chapters at a time, hoping the effect of the story would make readers feel so bad about slavery that they would rally to the abolitionist cause. Many people, reading *Uncle Tom's Cabin* installment by installment, did become convinced that nothing could be worse than living in slavery on a southern plantation.

None of the abolitionists, who devoted their energy to abolishing slavery, expected a perfect world when the book itself was published in 1852. But they certainly hoped that the book would be influential. It was. Of all the novels published that year, it was the top seller on both sides of the Atlantic. Its popularity was good news for the abolitionists. Harriet Beecher Stowe's wish had come true.

EXERCISE 27-1, page 84

Suggested revision:

Most Americans today don't realize that the American democratic system did not always include African Americans and women. The constitutional amendments passed after the Civil War granted former slaves and all native-born African American men full voting rights, but the new amendments ignored women. Women had to wait much longer—more than half a century—to be given the right to vote.

Some individual states allowed women to vote as early as 1900, but by 1910 women activists decided to focus their energy on a federal amendment. When Woodrow Wilson became president in 1913, women demonstrated along the inauguration route, marching and holding signs demanding the vote for women. Then in 1917, Alice Paul and a militant faction of the suffrage movement picketed the White House and even chained themselves to fences. When they were threatened and attacked by male mobs, police ignored the men and arrested the women. In prison, the women endured filthy cells, force-feeding when they went on a hunger strike, and ill treatment. Some women were restrained for many hours in uncomfortable positions with their arms high over their heads. One

angry official repeatedly asked a doctor to declare one or more of the women insane. (The doctor refused.)

President Wilson was a man with major problems—a war abroad and women fighting for their rights at home. At first he tolerated the women picketers; he even sent coffee out to them. Then he just wanted the women to lay down their signs and banners and go home. But the increasing pressure from moderate and radical voices in the movement as well as public outrage over the women's prison treatment finally forced Wilson to support a constitutional amendment for women's voting rights.

EXERCISE 27-5, page 88

Suggested revision:

Almost everyone has heard about Aesop's fables, but most people know very little about Aesop himself. Most of what we know about Aesop is a mixture of hearsay and conjecture. We do know that he was a slave in Greece. One theory is that before he came to Greece he had lived in Ethiopia for most of his life and that "Aesop" is a much-shortened form of "the Ethiopian."

Aesop was not a storyteller then, though he would have loved to speak well enough to tell a good story. He stuttered so badly that he did not even try to talk. In one story we learn, however, that he *could* communicate. A neighbor brought a gift of figs to Aesop's master. Greatly pleased, the master planned to enjoy the figs after his bath and directed that they be put in a cool place until he was ready. While the master was bathing, the overseer and his friends ate the figs. When the master discovered the loss of his figs, the other slaves placed the blame on Aesop. They knew that if Aesop were able to speak, he could defend himself, but they did not fear this stammering slave.

The master ordered that Aesop be flogged, but Aesop got the master to delay punishment briefly. After drinking a glass of warm water, Aesop ran his fingers down his throat and vomited only water. Pointing at the overseer, he made gestures that the overseer and his friends should do as he had done. They drank the water, ran their fingers down their throats—and vomited figs.

Although Aesop's cleverness saved him from a flogging, it also made an enemy of the overseer. Aesop discovered a basic truth about life: Being right doesn't always help one to make friends.

EXERCISE 28-1, page 93

Suggested revision:

Immigrants have come to the United States from all over the world. Initially, new settlers were mostly European, Irish, or English. By the early twentieth century, many Asians had taken a frightening boat trip across the Pacific to get here. Usually the men came first. After they had made enough money for passage, their wives and children were brought over. All thought that if they worked hard, they would make a good life, as earlier European immigrants had done. A large number of Chinese and Japanese settled in the western part of the United States.

These new immigrants worked on the railroads and in the mines. American businesses recruited Chinese labor because American workers would not accept the wages that were paid. Why did workers decide to come to America anyway? Somehow the idea got started that America was a "golden mountain" where people could pick up gold nuggets after an easy climb. Once they got here, most immigrants worked hard because they hoped to make enough money to bring relatives over to America too.

Before and during World War II, many Germans who had been persecuted by Hitler escaped to America. After the war, thousands of "displaced persons" were welcomed by the United States. Later, refugees from Asia, Africa, Latin America, and the Caribbean wanted to be accepted. Franklin D. Roosevelt once said, "All of our people all over the country, except the pure-blooded Indians, are immigrants or descendants of immigrants." If Roosevelt were alive today, he would know that his statement is still true.

EXERCISE 29-1, page 102

Suggested revision:

People all over the world have stories that are part of their culture. Many cultures have a creation story that explains how the world came to be. Sometimes the story tells how a single piece of the world got its characteristics. It is not surprising that these stories exist; what is surprising is how similar the stories are. Consider the Cinderella story, for example. Cinderella has different names in different places, and details of her adventure are not the same; but the basic story echoes around the world.

In Egypt, she is called Rhodopis (the word means "rosy cheeked"). Rhodopis is a Greek slave in an Egyptian home. She does not have eyes or hair like anyone else in the home. Her green eyes look quite different from the eyes of the other girls. Their dark, straight hair almost never gets tangled; her yellow, curly hair blows into a tangled mass around her face. Her light-skinned face turns red and burns when she is in the sun too long. When someone calls her "Rosy Rhodopis," she blushes, and her cheeks become rosier.

Unable to make friends with the other girls, Rhodopis turns to the animals in the nearby woods and streams for companionship.

EXERCISE 30/31-1, page 106

Suggested revision:

A descendant of one of the earliest immigrants to North America played a pivotal role in helping later Americans explore their country. There were tribes of American Indians living all over what is now the United States. Each tribe had its own language and customs. Some tribes raided others and took prisoners who then became the raiding tribes' slaves. That is what happened to a young Shoshone girl now known as Sacagawea.

This girl, like many young girls, had a nickname, "He-toe." "He-toe" was the sound a local bird made, and the girl's movements were as swift as that bird's. When a raiding party of Hidatsas easily captured this young girl, they named her Sacagawea—"bird woman." Sacagawea was about twelve years old. The frightened young girl did not try to escape but accepted her role and worked for her captors. In [*or* After] a few months, she had acquired a reputation for good sense and good work.

The tribe married Sacagawea to a white man, Toussaint Charbonneau; she was his second wife. Soon pregnant, this typical Indian wife did the chores and left all decisions to her husband; but inwardly, she longed to explore new places and meet new people. She may have been controlled by her husband, but she never missed a chance to learn whatever she could.

When white men appeared, many Indians were curious. Sacagawea had never seen a man with yellow hair—or red hair. Nor had she ever seen a black man. All these men were trying to get to the "Big Water" far to the west. They would have to cross mountains that they had not even seen yet. They needed horses and guides that the Shoshone could supply and an interpreter who could speak the Shoshone language. Imagine their surprise when this interpreter, whom they had hoped to find, turned out to be a woman—an attractive young Shoshone woman.

EXERCISE 32/33-1, page 113

If a boy wanted to join the football team at Carlisle Indian School, he had to go through a difficult test. Any boy who wanted to be on the team had to stand at one of the goal lines; all the first-string players stood around the field. When the ball was punted to the new boy, he had to catch it and try to get all the way to the other end zone with it. The team members tried to stop him before he could get very far. Only a few players had ever gotten as far as the fifty-yard line, so "Pop" Warner, coach at the Carlisle Indian School, considered it a good test.

One day a quiet Native American boy surprised Pop. The boy caught the ball, started running, wheeled away from the first players who tried to stop him, shook off the others, and ran the ball all the way to the opposite goal line. Convinced that the player's success was an accident, the coach ordered him to run the play again. Brusquely, the coach spoke to the players and reminded them that this workout was supposed to be tackling practice. Jim, the nineteen-year-old six-footer, simply said, "Nobody tackles Jim." Then he ran the ball to the goal line a second time.

Well, almost no one tackled Jim Thorpe successfully for many years. Life itself got him down and made him fumble more often than his football opponents did, but he was usually able to recover and go on. The first blow was the death of his twin brother while the two boys were still in grade school. This tragedy was followed by others; by the time Jim was twenty-five, his mother and his father had also died. They left him a Native American heritage: His father was half Irish and half Native American, and his mother was the granddaughter of a famous Native American warrior named Chief Black Hawk.

Fortunately or unfortunately, along with his Native American heritage came great pride and stoicism. That pride kept him silent when the greatest blow of all came: He was forced to return the Olympic medals he had won in 1912 because he was declared to be not an amateur. He dealt stoically with his personal tragedies. When infantile paralysis struck his son, Jim Thorpe disappeared for a few days to deal with the tragedy alone. His stoicism also saw him through a demotion to the minor leagues and sad years of unemployment and poverty before his death.

Even death's tackle may not have been totally successful: After Jim Thorpe's death, his Olympic medals were returned, and a town was named after him.

EXERCISE 34-1, page 121

When Cheryl Toussaint came in second in a race she had never planned to run, she started on a road that led to the Olympics and a world record.

Cheryl began running almost by accident one day when she went to watch a city-sponsored track meet in Brooklyn, New York. During the preliminaries, the officials announced an "open" race; it was one that anyone could enter. Cheryl wanted to enter, but she was dressed in a skirt and sandals. Four things made her run: One [*or* one] friend traded shoes with her, another let her borrow jeans, several called her "chicken" if she didn't run, and one girl dared her to run. Coming in second in that race led this teenager to many places, including Munich, Germany; Toronto, Canada; and Montreal, Canada.

There were, however, many races to run and lessons to learn. Cheryl joined the all-female Atoms Track Club, and she began training under Coach Fred Thompson. Like most coaches, Fred had his own way of testing newcomers. He watched new runners carefully; however, he gave them no special attention. Instead, he just gave them orders one after another. He would tell Cheryl to run laps, perform exercises, and repeat practice starts; at the same time, he would never comment on how she performed. If the newcomers endured the hard, time-consuming workouts without encouragement or praise, Thompson was sure that they were ready for real coaching.

Cheryl quit after two months; for six more months, she stayed away from the club. During that time, she thought about her attitude toward work, her poor record at school, her pleasure in running, and her lack of goals. When she returned to the club, Thompson welcomed her back. Coach Thompson knew how special Cheryl was. He not only convinced her she was college material but also pushed her to achieve the highest goal of the amateur athlete—competing in the Olympics.

EXERCISE 35-1, page 125

In 1951, Althea Gibson broke the color barrier in women's tennis and became admired all over the world. No one who knew her as a teenager would have predicted her success. By the time Althea Gibson reached her teens, her record showed three indications of trouble: running away from home, dropping out of school, and losing the one job she had been able to find.

To survive in her neighborhood, Althea depended on a small welfare allowance, occasional handouts, and plain old luck. She listed her skills as the following: good bowler, great two-on-two basketball player, and fast paddleball player. Even after she began playing tennis and moving in upper-class Harlem society, she resented the efforts of the society ladies to improve her. They busied themselves with tasks such as correcting her manners and restricting her behavior. Looking back, she summed up her earlier attitude: She [or she] said she hadn't been ready to study about "how to be a fine lady." At eighteen, she finally got a waitressing job, a congenial roommate, and a good friend.

EXERCISE 36-1, page 129

During the 1990 troubles in Panama, American television and newspaper reporters had an exciting piece of news. They reported that for the first time American female soldiers had been engaged in actual combat. Acting as her soldiers' leader, Captain Linda Bray led her troops into combat. Names of two additional women who were involved in combat, Staff Sergeant April Hanley and Private First Class Christina Proctor, were reported in the newspapers. Theirs were the only names reported, although other women also took part in the fighting.

It wasn't the first time an American woman had fought in an American battle, but it's not likely that many people are aware of that fact. The Civil War had its female fighters too. Loreta Janeta Velazquez fought for the Confederates in the Civil War after her husband's death. Like many other women whose husbands were killed in that war, she must have asked herself, "Who's going to take his place in battle?" The decision to fight was hers alone. Someone is sure to ask how that was possible, especially in those days. Military identification was not very sophisticated in the 1860s. Someone's willingness to fight was that person's major qualification, and each fighting unit needed to replace its losses as fast as possible. Velazquez simply disguised herself in men's clothing, found a troop needing replacements, and joined the fight. Loreta Janeta Velazquez was Linda Bray's Civil War predecessor.

EXERCISE 37-1, page 133

1. The doctor answered, "You can do nothing but pray."
2. When the bandages were removed and the shades were opened to let in the bright sunlight, the doctor asked, "What do you see?"
3. "Nothing," said the boy. "I see nothing."
4. The village priest said, "I have recently seen a remarkable school." He had just returned from a trip to Paris.
5. "In this school," he added, "blind students are taught to read."
6. "You didn't say 'read,' did you?" asked the boy's father.
7. The boy responded to the priest's words as if they were a trick of some kind: "Now you are joking with me. How can such a thing be possible?"
8. The boy, Louis, thought it would be great fun to visit that school someday.
9. His father promised, "We will go soon, Louis."
10. And so it happened that ten-year-old Louis Braille entered the National Institute for Blind Youths and began the long effort to erase the fear people had of even the word "blind." [Or the word *blind* can be italicized, without quotation marks.]

EXERCISE 38-1, page 137

After Louis Braille invented his new system that would allow blind people to read and write, he tested it thoroughly. Students and faculty of the National Institute for Blind Youths were excited at how easily they could master it. They encouraged Louis to demonstrate the system to the French educational authorities, who made the rules for the institute. Louis agreed to do so.

When Louis held the demonstration, all went well. What excitement he and his friends felt! But the authorities would not recommend that the institute adopt Louis's new system. Why didn't the French authorities recognize the advantages

of Braille's system? Did they have a vested interest in the old system of teaching the blind? Or a real doubt about the new system? Whatever their reasons, they delayed the pleasures of reading for thousands of people. In addition, a new director, Dr. Pignier, even outlawed the use of the system at the institute for four years.

Although unhappy and disheartened, Braille never gave up; he knew his system would enable the blind to read.

EXERCISE 39-1, page 142

The most famous woman in America is Miss Liberty—a 450,000-pound, 154-foot resident of New York City. For people all over the world, the Statue of Liberty symbolizes America. Yet the idea for the statue came not from America, England, or even New York itself—but from France. Three men can claim credit for the construction of Miss Liberty: (1) Frédéric-Auguste Bartholdi, sculptor; (2) Alexandre-Gustave Eiffel, structural engineer; and (3) Richard Morris Hunt, architect. France gave the statue to the United States, and the United States provided the pedestal on which it stands.

Two Americans contributed significantly to the statue. The first was Joseph Pulitzer, then owner and publisher of the *New York World* and a Russian immigrant. He led several fund-raising efforts and urged every American to give what he or she could to help build the pedestal. The second American who contributed significantly was Emma Lazarus. She wrote the famous lines on the bronze plaque inside the statue. Her three-word title "The New Colossus" (which means "huge statue") alludes to a statue built in the harbor of Rhodes in ancient Greece. The most quoted lines from "The New Colossus" are probably these: "Give me your tired, your poor, / Your huddled masses yearning to breathe free."

EXERCISE 40/41/42-1, page 147

Everyone has heard of Christopher Columbus, but not many people know much about him. Most people learn that he discovered America in AD 1492. Some people know that he had three ships, and they might be able to name them. (The ships were the *Niña*, the *Pinta*, and the *Santa María*.) A few people might even remember that Columbus thought he had found the Indies. And those with great self-confidence might be willing to guess at the number of trips he made to his Indies. (It was four.) Probably no one could tell you his favorite word, *adelante*.

If they were asked what Columbus was trying to prove with his expensive journey, most people would reply that he was trying to prove that the world is round. They would be wrong. If they were asked what Columbus meant by the term *Indies*, they would most likely say "India." They would be wrong again. If they were asked what Columbus's rank was, they would most likely say "captain." They would be wrong again. If they were asked what his sailors feared most, a number of them would reply, "They feared that the boats would fall off the edge of the earth." And they would be wrong again.

Isn't it strange that people can be so ignorant about a well-known man like Columbus?

EXERCISE 43/44/45-1, page 151

Suggested revision:

Columbus's return to Spain from his first exploration was difficult. The *Niña* and the *Pinta* were separated, the *Niña* almost sank, and the governor on the island of Santa María had put Columbus's whole crew in jail. It seemed a miracle that both boats survived their journeys and arrived in the harbor at Palos on the same day.

As difficult as that return was, the reception at court quite made up for it. Columbus certainly made an all-out effort to impress the court, the city, and the entire country. Lavishly attired, he received a grand welcome as he led his entourage into Barcelona, the Spanish capital. It must have been a sight to behold: a procession like none Barcelona had ever seen before. Leading the parade was a gaudily bedecked horse carrying Columbus, followed by six captive "Indians" and all the crew. Everyone but Columbus was carrying boxes, baskets, and cages full of interesting and exotic items.

When the group reached the throne room, King Ferdinand and Queen Isabella stood up to greet Columbus formally and admire his apron-covered captives. Columbus asked the royal couple to accept gifts of plants, shells, darts, thread, and gold. As intrigued as they were with the other gifts, King Ferdinand and Queen Isabella basically wanted the gold. Luckily, Columbus had collected enough of it to satisfy them.

By the end of his first week home, Columbus had such prestige that everyone wanted to accommodate the wishes of the Italian sailor at the court of Spain. Columbus had no doubt that he would receive a commission for a second voyage of exploration or even colonization.

EXERCISE 46-1, page 157

readers, N; are, MV; of, P; its, ADJ *or* PN; and, C; or, C; formal, ADJ; starts, MV; simply, ADV; with, P; should, HV; everyone, PN; about, P; certain, ADJ; when, C; them, PN; acts, MV; government, N; bold, ADJ; been, HV

EXERCISE 47-1, page 166

group, S; had, V; problem, DO; they, S; went, V; They, S; gave, V; paintings, IO; bursts, DO; lovers, S; were surprised, V; artists, S; made, V; scenes, DO; bright, OC; would pour, V; sunshine, S; Were, V; paintings, S; bright, SC; cheerful, SC; painters, S; are admired, V; forms, S; are, V; examples, SC; Both, S; showed, V; viewers, IO; objects, DO

EXERCISE 48-1, page 172

Verbal phrases: Drawing colorful pictures; To decorate her room; Encouraging her artistic interest; Studying, working, and making new friends; to follow her own vision; Rewarded and acclaimed

Prepositional phrases: From her earliest years; of pretty rocks, shells, and fabric pieces; for only eleven years; to her family home; At times; During Louise Nevelson's busiest and most exciting years; with either the critics or the public; throughout the art world

Subordinate clauses: that she needed; who was a wealthy New York businessman; while his mother studied abroad; whether she had done the right thing; that she had made the right decision

EXERCISE 49-1, page 178

Simple; Complex: Even if they are not sports fans (subordinate clause); Complex: what Jackie Robinson did on the ball field, what he did off the field (subordinate clauses); Compound; Complex: Because the football team was not integrated (subordinate clause); Complex: While he was still in the army—and a second lieutenant to boot (subordinate clause); Simple; Compound-complex: when he refused to go to the back (subordinate clause); Complex: When his case came up (subordinate clause); Complex: that followed (subordinate clause)